D0545129

99

Businesses to Start at Home

WITHDRAWN
FROM
STOCK

KIM BENJAMIN

crimson

4685 369

This edition first published in Great Britain 2009 by
Crimson Publishing, a division of Crimson Business Ltd
Westminster House
Kew Road
Richmond
Surrey
TW9 2ND

© Kim Benjamin 2009

The right of Kim Benjamin to be identified as the author of this work has been asserted by
her in accordance with the Copyright, Designs and Patents Act, 1988.

All rights reserved. No part of this publication may be reproduced, transmitted in any form
or by any means, or stored in a retrieval system without either the prior written permission
of the publisher, or in the case of reprographic reproduction a licence issued in accordance
with the terms and licences issued by the CLA Ltd.

A catalogue record for this book is available from the British Library.

ISBN 978 1 85458 475 5

Printed and bound by MPG Books Ltd, Bodmin

Contents

Introduction

Why start a business from home?

There's no escaping the fact that we are living in uncertain times. In the last year, financial markets have been in turmoil, creating a tough economic climate where housing prices have plunged and retail sales have experienced an unprecedented decline. The outlook for the year ahead offers little comfort, with many predictions pointing towards the UK economy worsening before it gets better.

Tough economic times, however, are often the impetus to launch a home-based business. The recession is placing many jobs under threat, meaning that a greater number of people are likely to be weighing up their employment options and considering whether it would be better to go it alone. While it's undeniably harder to raise finance in the current climate, many home-based businesses can be launched with very little start-up capital, and you could be saving money at the same time.

For one thing, overheads are considerably reduced as you don't need to pay for premises or for transport costs to and from a place of work. You can also claim an element of your utility bills back against tax. Working from home also offers you the option of starting small and testing the market, lessening the potential for risk.

There are varied motivations, too. Some start a home-based business to earn a second, part-time income while others want the ability to exercise more control over their working life and personal commitments. Many people who start a business from home may also be dissatisfied with their current status as an employee. They may be worried about their future prospects at their current employer's, or keen to challenge themselves with a home-based business to increase their sense of self-esteem and achievement.

The reasons above, coupled with recent improvements in technology, have made working from home not only possible, but often easier than working in an office. High-speed broadband, Blackberries and PDAs (personal digital assistant) have all made working remotely second nature and competition among technology providers is fierce, offering a wide range of prices and products to choose from. There's no reason why opting for a home-based business should have a negative impact on your ability to be successful.

Of course, there are issues to be aware of when working from home, such as your levels of motivation and the reactions of any family members or friends who may share your space with you. If you have been used to working as part of a team or having people around you, having to rely on yourself and you alone can be a difficult experience to adjust to. A home-based business can also create an atmosphere of loneliness – with just you in control, a feeling of isolation can hit hard. You'll also be responsible for everything in the business – from marketing, to business development to raising funds – and for some this responsibility can be quite a lot to take in.

Choosing your business

Home-based businesses have come a long way from being viewed as something that people would occasionally dabble in to being recognised as businesses that can make some serious money and offer high levels of job satisfaction. There are many businesses that you can start from home, based either on your past experience, after having completed a training course or completely from scratch. You may also have an existing hobby that you want to make more permanent.

Some of the most popular home-based businesses will come as no surprise to you – they are those we traditionally think of as being run from home, including childcare, crafts, interior design and music lessons. In recent years, however, other businesses have become equally popular from being based at home, including accountancies, financial advice consultancies and travel agencies. The growth of the internet has also prompted many to consider starting a business from home, using either an eBay business model or by establishing their own online retail shops.

In many cases, you'll only need a computer, internet connection and phone to get started, in others you'll need a little bit of capital to give you that jump start. While you won't make millions overnight, you'll certainly be rewarded in other ways, such as job satisfaction, flexible working hours, the chance to learn on the job, and the opportunity to tackle some new skills.

The businesses in this book are split into eight different sections. Each will guide you through some of the many options available, giving you information on what the job entails, what the appeal is, what skills you need, potential income, how much it costs to set up, red tape issues, the advantages and disadvantages, tips for success, prospects for growth, and useful contacts.

The lure of online

If you fancy yourself as the next Google or Amazon, then an internet-based business could appeal to you. Whatever your reason for considering starting a home-based business, the internet provides countless opportunities, ranging from online retail, to web design to consultancy in areas such as search engine optimisation. With only the need for an internet connection, you could run a business from home and other locations, and tap into a global customer base at the touch of a key. This section includes setting up an eBay business and online retail.

What's the appeal?

- Low overheads and start-up costs

- You can work on the business at nights and weekends, leaving you free to continue a day job

- You can start off small and decide at a later stage whether to commit to it

Home is where the business is

These are busy times for those involved in the house and garden industries. In a time of recession, an increasing number of people are turning to opportunities in this sector. Property prices have plunged, making it harder for people to move up the property ladder, consequently, many are investing in improving and converting their current properties. Even if people have maintenance work that is not pressing, they are often reluctant to let this lie, as the problem can worsen if left and ultimately become more expensive to maintain or repair. This section covers jobs ranging from handyman to house-sitter to wardrobe organiser.

What's the appeal?

- The hours can be flexible and there are plenty of opportunities for fresh air

- Marketing costs can be reduced – many of the jobs featured rely on word of mouth for referrals

- There are plenty of training courses available to help you get your skills up to speed

Health boom

Obesity levels in the UK have been in the public eye for some time, with celebrity chefs such as Jamie Oliver fronting campaigns to increase the nation's health and fitness levels, particularly those of children. Opportunities in healthcare are therefore proving attractive, with a myriad of roles ranging from personal trainer to yoga instructor. If you are keen to undertake some further study and enjoy learning, then training in more specialised fields such as physiotherapy and osteopathy may prove attractive options. The fitness and personal services section also covers jobs such as life coach, marriage counsellor and nail technician.

What's the appeal?

- It's a great way to stay in shape

- Some careers, such as physiotherapy, involve several years of training so you can invest in new skills for the long term

- You can make a genuine difference to people's lives

Children and animals

Never work with children or animals, or so the saying goes. These two areas, however, can provide some lucrative home-based business opportunities. If you have a young family, for example, childcare will allow you to balance your work time with your own children, and is a good choice for parents who are already experienced in caring for their kids. And while consumer spend is being reined back, the same can't be said for the amount of money being spent on pet grooming and pet supplies. According to figures released in 2008 from research company Mintel, the market for pet accessories has grown by between 3% and 4% year on year, with beautifying treatments and eco-friendly products boosting growth prospects. In these two sections, we cover opportunities ranging from childcare to setting up a kids' football team to dog walking.

What's the appeal?

- A job in childcare attracts a good level of government support

- Working with animals will keep you fit

- The jobs can be quite sociable, combating feelings of isolation

Professional services

Launching a home-based business in this area appeals to many people. The range of jobs on offer – from tuition to writing to consulting to bookkeeping – offers people the opportunity to use existing skills in a more flexible manner than they would be able to do as company employees. While the potential income to be made varies from role to role, earnings can be quite lucrative, and are a key factor prompting many people to become self-employed in this area.

What's the appeal?

- Many of the jobs in this section can be easily run from home but involve visiting clients now and again, combining the best of both a home-based business and a workplace

- You can achieve high levels of personal satisfaction

- It can be a lucrative source of income

Creative services

If you've ever thought of turning a hobby into a business, then now could be the right time. Creative skills such as crafts, sewing repairs, making greeting cards and cake making can give you an opportunity to combine a love of doing something with making money. Actress Jane Asher, for example, used to love making cakes as a child and spent hours creating novelty cakes in the shape of animals and fairytale characters for her three children. A friend suggested she publish a book of her designs and this led to the opening of her own shop, which has established a reputation as a bespoke cake maker.

What's the appeal?

- You can start off small and weigh up the demand before investing further

- Creating something from scratch can be immensely satisfying

- Many of the items you create will be unique

That's entertainment

With the current state of the economy there might not be too many opportunities to celebrate, but working in entertainment, such as event planning, organising children's parties, mobile DJing and providing photography are all jobs where much of the demand is likely to be in the evenings or at weekends. As such, starting a home-based business in the entertainment sector can help you earn a second income, giving you the flexibility to fit around other commitments.

What's the appeal?

- There is a sense of fun attached to the work

- Much of the work will take place in the evenings and at weekends, so you can combine this work with other commitments

● The job involves a lot of customer liaison, helping to reduce any potential feelings of loneliness or isolation

Need to know

Whichever home-based business you choose to start, there are no set rules as to how to go about it, but there are some steps you can take that are common to all. Check out our tips below to help you get your home-based business off to a flying start.

Top tips for home-based businesses

● Separating home and work life is crucial

● Ensure you take short breaks – it will help to boost your levels of concentration

● Turn your office phone off at the end of the day

● Keep records of your utilities use so you can claim an element of this back

● You might not be based at home all the time so shop around for utilities and communications suppliers to ensure you get the best deal for your needs

● If you incur travel expenses, assess how much you can claim back and whether you can charge some to your customers, but remember to factor this in your costs as you need to pay these up front

● Build up a good relationship with your bank manager – many home-based businesses face seasonal peaks and troughs and you may need a helping hand with finance

● Check rules for planning permission and whether you need to pay business rates – this will depend on what area of your home you are using and how you expect to use it

1

Online

Profile – Online retail

Who: Holly Tucker

What she does: Online retail

Where: London

Set up business: 2005, launched a year later

Initial start-up costs: £140,000

Holly Tucker describes her business as a market-tailer – a mix between an online retailer and a marketplace and a gift site for yourself and others. Not On The High Street.com, set up in 2005, showcases products from small businesses that can be found in urban markets, country fairs or tiny villages – anywhere apart from on the high street. The site offers sellers a dedicated home page and URL, product pages with images and copy and inclusion in marketing and PR campaigns.

Inspiration came from Holly's previous jobs and a love for small businesses. Having worked for big names such as Condé Nast and Publicis, she started a business called 'Your Local Fair' in 2004, a list of local events in London where products from many small businesses were available to the general public.

"I've seen many boutiques on the high-street close down and give way to yet another coffee shop," she says. "These type of shops are an untapped market so there was a real need for people to find small businesses like these."

Tucker and her business partner Sophie Cornish ploughed personal savings, a bank loan (£20,000) and money from friends and family into the business. Most of the start-up costs were swallowed up by the website design.

'We had to build it from scratch and create a bespoke content management system as we were dealing with multiple partners and products,' recalls Holly. 'There was nothing out there like it so we had nothing to copy. We set up the business in our dining rooms and would swap houses each week. In early 2006, we invested in office space.'

Setting up the business in this way gave Holly the flexibility to juggle her work with family life and other commitments, as she had a three-month-old son at the time, although it did mean long hours – she was working till midnight and getting up at 5am.

Building the website was the hardest part of setting up an online retail business, as the technology Holly and Sophie envisioned using was not available so they had to invent it as they went along. Holly had already built up numerous contacts from her previous job – she had a list of 600 businesses that would be appropriate to approach to join the site. But she didn't rest on her laurels and continued to look for new ways of generating leads, visiting events for networking opportunities and sourcing names from articles and adverts in magazines.

'We worked forty weekends in our first year – it was like going on a hike that gets steeper and steeper until you eventually reach a sheer cliff face,' Holly says. 'We were constantly learning, pushing ourselves and taking on board new ideas, asking ourselves how much pain we could handle. We made things up as we went along. Now that we are established and have a reputation, we have the opportunity to educate shoppers about our business.'

Holly believes that creating an online marketplace and sectors (such as gifts for weddings) has been one of the best aspects of the work, together with dealing with a diverse product range. The site caters to a female audience and the products are original and of a high quality, with the aim of offering unusual gifts and a personal service to customers.

There are currently around 800 businesses listed on the site, and the company deals with about 20 applications a day and now has to turn some businesses away. Revenues are generated by small businesses paying a one-off joining fee of £500 and the site takes a commission of 23% on each product sold.

According to Holly, the business is on course to record its first profit in early 2009. She says that start-up capital is an important consideration for anyone starting an online business as the costs really depend on what you are trying to achieve and what functionality the website will have. The business had a finance director from day one and although Holly says they had little difficulty in securing finance from banks and friends and family, looking back, she might have approached things differently. If she could do it all again, she says she would take the money she got to start with and multiply it by five.

'One of the biggest challenges has been keeping positive and remaining confident with the financial side of the business – we did not raise enough money to start with,' she says. 'You think it's impossible that you would need such a huge amount of money to start a business, but it will be half the amount you actually need. Ensure you get an overdraft arranged or at least have it agreed in principle. For an online business, it's also crucial to get your technology right from the start, so invest time in planning this. And always have confidence in what you are doing.'

Online retail

What is it?

Selling goods and products over the internet – online retail is often referred to as an e-commerce business. You'll be creating a website to display your goods and setting up facilities to enable people to purchase goods and pay for them online. You'll also need to think about ways of marketing your site using search engine optimisaton to ensure that potential customers know about your business.

What's the appeal?

It's simple to start up – all you need is access to an internet connection and some business acumen.

What skills do I need?

Knowing your audience and your product are vital to success so research skills are a must. You don't need to have any technical expertise, but marketing and sales skills will be valuable. You will want to strike a balance between a site that looks good, and gets users to return, but which doesn't cost the earth to build.

What does it cost?

You'll need to fork out for a web address (£25) a hosting service (between £40 and £50 a year, although depends on the size of the site) and a website build. It can cost as little as £500 to build a website, or as much as many thousands, depending on your needs and what functionalities you want to incorporate.

What can I earn?

This depends on the type of products you are selling, how much you buy them for, and at what price you sell them on.

Any red tape?

The Consumer Protection (Distance Selling) Regulations apply to any business that sells products online, via mail order, telephone or fax, so ensure you are up to date with the latest regulations. You'll also need to display your contact details clearly on your website.

Prospects for growth

These might be worrying times for the economy, but e-commerce and online retail sales are still growing at a reasonable rate, as more shoppers turn to the internet rather than spend money travelling to retail stores.

Tips for success

Carve out a niche or focus on a specialist category and gauge demand. In online retail, you'll be competing with the likes of Tesco as well as smaller players, so selling something that is niche and desirable will get you noticed. Offer incentives to build up a customer base, such as giving discounts to customers who refer a friend.

Pros

Low overhead and start-up costs and you can work on the business at nights and on weekends, leaving you free to work at a day job. You can start off small, work on it part-time or even view it as a hobby before you decide whether to commit to it.

Cons

Websites don't get indexed by search engines overnight, so it can take time for traffic to build so you'll need to look at other ways to market your business in the early days.

Useful contact

Resources and industry information: http://econsultancy.com

eBay

What is it?

Internet auction website eBay is one of the fastest growing retail phenomena of our time. The opportunities offered by an eBay business stretch way beyond selling unwanted bric-a-brac or discarded Christmas presents. Growing numbers of people are making healthy second incomes by buying items and selling them online on eBay for profit.

What's the appeal?

The simplicity of setting up an eBay business is a big attraction for many people.

What skills do I need?

Commitment – making an eBay business work is not easy but it can be extremely rewarding. The ability to build trust and offer excellent customer service will improve your prospects. Negotiation skills come in handy too when you are buying stock.

What does it cost?

You don't really need anything other than a computer and storage space. Your biggest challenge will be finding plenty of low cost products you can sell at a profit. It costs between 15p and £2 to list an item on eBay, depending on the opening value or reserve price of the item. The site takes a slice of the selling fee once an item is sold, depending on how much the item is worth.

What can I earn?

There is no sure-fire way to make a profit, but by sourcing goods at a low price and selling them at the going rate, with prompt delivery, you should begin building up your takings.

Any red tape?

To be able to open a shop, you need to have a PayPal account, an international online transactions facility, plus a minimum score of five positive feedback reviews.

Alternatively, if you don't have a PayPal account, you need a minimum score of 10. You also need an automatic payment method on file to pay seller fees (credit card, debit card, bank account). There are various items which are not allowed to be sold, such as animals, alcohol and offensive material.

Prospects for growth

Research the eBay market in your particular sector as well as on the internet to see what the competition is doing and what is being offered. Find a point of difference that will set you apart from your competitors.

Tips for success

The most obvious and efficient way to accumulate products is to buy them in bulk from wholesalers. If you strike an agreement with a wholesaler, you should be able to get a constant supply of warehouse stock for your new business. There are various options to make you stand out from the crowd, such as premium listings and titles in bold. Although these options do not cost much by themselves, it will add up if you are listing many items.

Pros

Starting an eBay business can be lucrative if done properly and you can work from home, choosing your own hours.

Cons

By their very nature auctions are unpredictable, but they are the only way to 'test the water' and see what kind of demand there is for your stock.

Useful contact

www.ebay.co.uk

Web design

What is it?

It involves using programming and design skills to build new websites and refresh existing ones. You'll be responsible for the layout, visual appearance and usability of a website and will be expected to liaise closely with clients during each project. You could be writing web pages using codes such as HTML and Javascript, sourcing images, testing the site for functionality and coming up with original designs.

What's the appeal?

Being able to take someone else's or your own vision from ideas to reality and seeing the finished product on the web.

What skills do I need?

The role encompasses graphic design skills and technical knowledge and you must enjoy learning new technologies and skills as the world of web design changes rapidly. As you will be liaising closely with clients, good communication skills are essential. Many web designers have a degree in new media or multimedia but this isn't essential. If you're starting from scratch you could take a training course in programming and design. You should also have knowledge of software packages such as Adobe Photoshop, used for basic layouts.

What does it cost?

You'll need a computer and internet connection and ideally access to packages such as Dreamweaver, Photoshop, Flash and Fireworks (£1,400).

What can I earn?

This varies depending on what work you will be doing. Some web designers charge by the page, others by the hour, where rates start at £30 but can go up to £90. Updates and changes for example, are typically charged at £20 an hour. Be very clear what expenses you will charge to the client. As a website design can go through several changes before completion, it could be worth adding a 10% contingency fee to more complex projects, to cover any changes that go beyond the contract.

Any red tape?

There is legislation and guidelines for website accessibility of which you should be aware. If you join a trade body, such as the UK Web Design Association, you will need to abide by their rules of conduct. Ensure you get professional indemnity insurance to protect against any problems.

Prospects for growth

There is a lot of competition but there are plenty of opportunities to tap into to expand your services, such as the IT departments of companies in the public and private sectors and web design agencies.

Tips for success

Web design is a fast-growing and competitive field so keep up to date with software and new technologies. Clients will be keen to see evidence of your ability, so build up a portfolio of your work that you can demonstrate at meetings.

Pros

It's a very creative job and offers much variety, as you will be working for a range of clients and industries.

Cons

Deadlines are part and parcel of web design so you could find yourself working late nights to complete projects. Communication problems can also be an issue so make sure you always understand what is expected of you.

Useful contacts

The UK Web Design Association: www.ukwda.org
British Computer Society: www.bcs.org

PC repair

What is it?

Maintaining and repairing computers and related equipment such as printers, routers and scanners. You could also be dealing with software upgrades, virus attacks and problems with internet connections, as well as carrying out routine testing to diagnose potential faults. You'll often be required to provide estimates for repairs.

What's the appeal?

You enjoy taking things apart, problem-solving and fixing. It's a job for those who like working with their hands and who have analytical minds.

What skills do I need?

A good knowledge of different types of hardware and software is essential, alongside bags of patience – you'll need to spend time with the devices before you can figure out the problem and fix it. If you haven't got a good enough working knowledge of PCs and related systems, there are many courses available that will help you to analyse faults and repair them.

What does it cost?

The cost of PC repair courses varies but budget around £400 for a six-month course, which takes you from beginner status to level 2, giving you the skills to upgrade computer systems and solve a range of problems. Basic computer repair kits cost from £20 and you might also need to invest in a PC cleaning kit (£18), a screw kit (£20) and other equipment depending on the nature of the repairs.

What can I earn?

This depends on the types of repair you carry out and the market you aim at: business or home users. You can charge per job – data recovery and software problems (£25) to more complex repairs such as rebuilds (£50) or per hour, starting from £25 to £30. Some repair businesses charge more for the first hour and then less after that, while some cap prices after a certain amount of time, such as four hours.

Any red tape?

Protect yourself with public liability and professional indemnity insurance. You'll also need to be aware of electrical safety issues.

Prospects for growth

Computers are a must for modern living so there is always demand for people qualified in PC repairs. Word-of-mouth recommendations are important in this line of work so emphasise reliability and professionalism.

Tips for success

Practise on an old PC first to ensure you know what the components are and how they work. Keep up to date with the latest trends as developments in computers and IT happen rapidly. Even if the work takes less than an hour to complete, stick to your minimum charging period of one hour and offer to carry out a general PC health check, for example, to use up the remainder of the time. This will show customers you are willing to go the extra mile and will help boost your reputation.

Pros

As a business, it needs relatively minimal start-up costs and depending on the hours you do, it's possible to generate a healthy income.

Cons

In order to increase your appeal, you might have to do call outs in the evening or at weekends, when most people are likely to be at home.

Useful contacts

Computer Technology Industry Association: www.comptia.org
British Computer Society: www.bcs.org.uk

Leabharlann
Contae na Midhe
4685 36 0

Online boutique

What is it?

A retail business run on the internet that specialises in exclusive, hard to find and often luxury designer clothes and accessories, many of which are from new designers or from abroad. Online boutiques specialise in a niche, such as bridal wear, vintage, handbags, jewellery, accessories and lingerie.

What's the appeal?

It's ideal for those who are obsessed with clothes, shopping and fashion trends and who like to put together different outfits and styles.

What skills do I need?

You don't need any specific qualifications but an in-depth knowledge of the fashion industry is essential and retail experience will also stand you in good stead. You'll need good negotiation skills too, to secure the best supplies at the best prices, as well as a good eye for the latest fashions and styles.

What does it cost?

You'll need to invest money in a website (which can cost from £500 to thousands more) and in marketing, which will vary depending on who you are targeting. This will include investing in email newsletters and search engine optimisation. To reduce your costs, you can consider keeping your stock at home.

What can I earn?

There's no sure-fire way of generating a profit as earnings depend on the type of products you stock, what price you negotiate with wholesalers, and at what price you decide to sell the products.

Any red tape?

Selling items over the internet, phone, by mail order or digital TV requires you to comply with the Consumer Protection (Distance Selling) Regulations. You must display certain information on your website, such as your business name, physical address and email address.

Prospects for growth

Consider services you can add to your online boutique to attract customers to come back and to gain new ones. For example you could expand to offering style appointments in people's homes or set up an online members' club, where people get access to exclusive offers.

Tips for success

Research the market thoroughly and decide who your target market is – this will help determine what products you stock. It's vital that you stay in touch with the latest trends and up-and-coming designers. Visit trade shows to spot new arrivals as well as to make contacts.

Pros

You can invest as little or as much time as you want in an online boutique, so it can easily fit round any other existing commitments.

Cons

There is a huge amount of competition in the online boutique area so it pays to do your research and see if you can spot an area that few are currently targeting, in terms of demographics and products.

Useful contact

Resources: www.fashioncapital.co.uk

SEO consultant

What is it?

SEO – search engine optimisation, involves specialising in website promotion and marketing with the aim of getting websites found and ranked higher up the search engines, making it easier for customers to find the websites. SEO can be done in two ways – organically (also called naturally) and by using pay-per-click, where you pay for certain keywords related to the content of your site.

What's the appeal?

It suits someone who is interested in all things Google and developments in search engines, with an aptitude for technical codes such as HTML (Hypertext Markup Language) and CSS (cascading style sheets).

What skills do I need?

You will need experience in content writing, the ability to research keywords, an in-depth understanding of how search engines work and good communication skills, as you will be working closely with website designers. Patience is vital too – SEO is not a one-off process as it takes time to develop and implement a strategy.

What does it cost?

Start-up costs are minimal. You will be carrying out the majority of the work at customers' premises so you will mainly be incurring travel costs. Invest in a laptop (from £300) so you can keep records of meetings.

What can I earn?

Rates vary depending on what type of service you are providing, what stage the optimisation is at and how much work you will be expected to complete. As a rough guide, consultants charge anywhere between £150 and £400 for a day rate, with fees per hour ranging from £20 to £50.

Any red tape?

There are no specific regulations but ensure you take out professional indemnity insurance.

Prospects for growth

Nurture links with website designers and consider offering your services to them – website design goes hand in hand with SEO so you might be able to generate future referrals. Word-of-mouth is one of the fastest ways to boost business in this area so tap into your contacts for referrals.

Tips for success

It can be quite a challenge getting a site ranked highly through natural search and it takes time, too, so many SEO consultants also offer pay-per-click SEO services. Prospective clients will want to see proof of your success so ensure you keep an up-to-date portfolio showing the 'before' and 'after' rankings of sites you have helped to optimise. SEO is a fast-moving industry, so keep up to date with the latest trends and developments to boost your profile.

Pros

Working in this area can be quite lucrative and as it is a fast-moving industry, there is likely to be plenty of variety.

Cons

Projects can take several months from start to finish, particularly if you specialise in organic or natural search, so it can take time to build your reputation and business.

Useful contact

Information and training: www.econsultancy.com
www.iab.net

2

House and garden

Profile – Handyman
Who: Tim Coombes
What he does: Handyman
Where: London
Set up business: 2006
Initial start-up costs: Around £1,000

Selling appliances and bar work might not be the most conventional route to becoming a handyman but it has certainly helped Tim Coombes, 35, to set up and grow a successful handyman and home maintenance service. Originally from Christchurch in New Zealand, Tim has a background in sales but says he enjoyed working with his hands and fixing things from an early age.

'When I was growing up in New Zealand, we had a garage and I was constantly building things,' he recalls. 'I then went into sales, worked in a galvanising plant and then came to the UK ten years ago, with the aim of saving money for travelling.'

Tim did shifts in a few bars before returning to New Zealand and saving enough money to return permanently to the UK, where he settled in Leeds, working as a drayman delivering beer to pubs. It certainly kept him fit as he was moving 40,000 tonnes of beer a day and starting work at 5am. He then moved to London where he swapped the early starts for late shifts in a bar, but he soon grew tired of this type of work and decided to build on his early handyman skills by working for a sash window and joinery business.

'I started off as a van driver and worked my way up to installing windows,' he says. 'I then saw an opportunity to go it alone providing windows and then branched out from there into general handyman work and home maintenance – the only things needed are a toolbox and some know-how.'

Looking back on his business now, Tim wishes he'd had the confidence to start earlier – he says he relied too much on getting a wage paid by someone else. One of the best aspects of being a handyman is meeting different people in a week's work, so a sociable personality and the ability to get on with people certainly help. All of his work is sourced through word-of-mouth and personal recommendations. Having built up a reputation, demand keeps him busy.

'There is a tendency in this job to work hard – I do the hours that are required and I'm lucky if I get a day off – time management is crucial,' he says. 'I work weekends too as I never know where or when the next job will come along.'

The financial reward of being a handyman is one of the best parts of the job, in Tim's opinion. He typically charges £170 a day for his work plus materials on top and as a general handyman, he can pretty much turn his hand to any odd job around the house that needs doing, from making cupboards, to putting up shelves to dealing with wiring.

'If you can do small jobs and put your own personal stamp on it, then your business can really get going. Don't be afraid of suggesting ideas to customers as they rely on you to help them turn their ideas into reality,' he believes. 'If you want to specialise in one area then it's probably a good idea to invest in training. I prefer to do small jobs as it keeps me moving and gives me flexibility – I can fit the work around my holidays, for example.'

The weather can sometimes affect work as most people attempt to tackle DIY and maintenance work in the summer so the winter months can prove to be a tougher time to find work. Tim says this makes it all the more important for handymen and women to be able to turn their hands to any job that needs doing around the house.

'Don't be afraid of getting advice from someone who knows an area better than you do – it means you get to learn on the job,' he says. 'If you are going to take on work that's a bit beyond your experience, make sure you know someone who can help out. I tend to bend over backwards to give customers what they want as good customer service is so important in this line of work.'

Public liability insurance is a must, which sets Tim back around £180 a year, and installing windows requires securing permission from local councils. Over the years, he has also built up a considerable tool collection that is stored in his garage – it's something Tim says one can add to as jobs are completed, so it's a good idea to hold back on investing too much up front until you can gauge demand and the type of work you want to specialise in. According to Tim, you would need to set aside around £1,000 to purchase a decent set of tools – the better quality you want, the more you will need to spend.

Cleaning

What is it?
It covers domestic cleaners, office cleaners, hospital and school cleaners as well as other niche businesses such as carpet, window and vehicle cleaners. As a domestic cleaner, you might find yourself cleaning a couple of properties every week.

What's the appeal?
It's an industry for perfectionists. Cleaning is all about making places look presentable and tidy so you need to be motivated enough to make things spotless.

What skills do I need?
The ability to instil confidence in your clients, so good customer relations skills are essential. Clients have to trust you implicitly if they're going to hand over the keys to their property, so first impressions count. You'll need good administrative skills too as you might be juggling several clients at once.

What does it cost?
The majority of the equipment you use may already be in the homes you clean so start-up costs can be minimal. Commercial contract cleaning will involve a bigger investment as you will need to buy equipment and this can be expensive, typically £200 upwards for an industrial vacuum cleaner for example. You'll spend some money on marketing your services.

What can I earn?
Average rates are around £6 an hour, although this is slightly higher in major cities.

Any red tape?
Cleaning involves handling potentially harmful chemicals so you will need to comply with acts such as the Chemicals Regulations, Dangerous Substances and Preparations (Safety) Regulations, Control of Substances Hazardous to Health Regulations and the Health and Safety at Work Act.

Prospects for growth?

If you are prepared to work weekends you could build the business up as well as charge more at these times. Word of mouth is vital to build up new clients so ask existing customers if they know anyone else in the area who requires a cleaner.

Tips for success

Do your research carefully – check out the areas you want to clean and see if people can afford to pay for someone to do their chores. Work locally and concentrate on a small geographical location so you can minimise the amount of time spent travelling. Check out the competition too and see how much they charge and what services they offer, so you can price your rates competitively.

Pros

For a domestic cleaning business, you need very little equipment or capital. Commercial cleaning is often carried out early in the mornings or late evenings so you can fit this round other jobs.

Cons

Clients can easily find fault with domestic cleaning services so you need to be able to deal with and respond to any negative feedback or comments.

Useful contacts

British Cleaning Council: www.britishcleaningcouncil.org
Cleaning and Support Services Association: www.cleaningindustry.org
British Institute of Cleaning Science: www.bics.org.uk/
Confederation of Cleaning Professionals: www.confcleanproof.org.uk

Window cleaning

What is it?

You wash windows and other glass surfaces on residential and commercial premises. It involves working at ground level and you might have to use ladders to reach upper floors, although many window cleaners now use ladderless systems such as water-fed poles. You might have to use power-operated platforms to reach windows in tower blocks.

What's the appeal?

Window cleaning is ideal for those who like working outdoors, want flexible hours, are safety-conscious and don't mind travelling.

What skills do I need?

You don't need any particular qualifications but there is a wide range of training courses available. It helps if you are physically fit, have a good sense of balance and like working with your hands. You should also enjoy working outdoors in all types of weather and ideally have a driving licence.

What can I earn?

The amount you can earn depends very much on where you will be working and how fast you can work. Generally, fees are based on a set number of windows or a fixed amount of time, with window cleaners charging between £20 and £30 an hour. You'll spend time travelling but average earnings can be around £200 a day.

What does it cost?

You'll need standard cleaning equipment such as a bucket, brush, cleaning solutions and cloths. Some larger window cleaning operations use pressurised water systems. Costs for water-fed poles start from £70.

Any red tape?

If you are planning to work at heights, you need rope access training and a certificate to show you are not putting yourself in danger. You'll also have to comply with the Work at Height Regulations which came into force in 2005. This involves ensuring that all work at height is properly planned and organised, assessing risk and using appropriate work equipment.

Prospects for growth

Good window cleaners are in demand and if you build up a reputation locally that does not require you to travel too much, you could fit many hours of work into one day.

Tips for success

Ensure you comply with safety regulations. Word of mouth can help generate new business, so make sure you communicate well with your customers.

Pros

You get plenty of fresh air, hours are very flexible and there are low start-up costs. You can choose where you want to work and there is no upper age limit.

Cons

The work can be physically tiring, demanding and repetitive and you might have to work longer hours in the summer months to compensate for reduced daylight in winter.

Useful contacts

Recognised training body: The British Window Cleaning Academy (BWCA) www.bwca.co.uk
Federation for Window Cleaners: www.nfmwgc.com
Educational body: The British Institute of Cleaning Science: www.bics.org.uk
Regulations: www.hse.gov.uk/falls/regulations.htm

House painting (exterior)

What is it?

Exterior house painting involves not only painting but preparing the surface prior to painting, using tools such as paint scrapers, and ensuring that the surface is clean, dry and free from grease, oils and flaking or loose paint.

What's the appeal?

You'll get to be outdoors and some of the work can be creative and artistic in nature, depending on customer needs.

What skills do I need?

There are no formal educational qualifications necessary but you will need to be good with your hands and it helps if you already have basic painting skills learned from painting interiors, for example. You will also need a head for heights and patience as exterior house painting is a job which demands attention to detail. There are also a range of painting and decorating courses you can enrol on, one provider is City & Guilds.

What can I earn?

Exterior house painters can charge by the hour, per sqm if doing a wall, or per house. They generally charge around £25 an hour or per sqm but this also depends on two factors – the height of the property and the current state of the exterior, which will also give you an idea of how many hours to dedicate to a property. You will also need to factor in the prices of paints, materials for surface preparation and any repairs and add this to what you charge.

What does it cost?

You'll need a few items to get started, such as ladders, brushes, cloths, paint scrapers, a putty knife and sandpaper or a sanding block. Depending on the quality you choose, these can cost anywhere between £500 and £1,000. Ideally, you should have a small van to transport the equipment easily and safely.

Any red tape?

Public liability cover is not a legal requirement but many customers may be wary about employing you without this. It will cover any accidental damage you do to a site or home during the job and will cover any injuries to anyone outside of your employment who is injured while you are carrying out work – for example, if you drop a paintbrush or pot from a height which injures a passer-by. You should also be aware of health and safety rules relating to uses of ladders and paints.

Prospects for growth

House exteriors are particularly vulnerable to the elements, so there is plenty of demand for exterior house painting.

Tips for success

As almost anyone can start an exterior house painting business, competition can be strong. Consider offering a few value-added services, such as cleaning gutters or windows to boost referrals and ask your customers to provide you with testimonials.

Pros

This job is ideal for those who like working outdoors and who enjoy methodical, detailed work.

Cons

The work can be slow, repetitive and tedious and you will need to put in longer hours over the summer months to compensate for bad weather and shorter daylight hours in winter. You will also need to be reasonably fit to both carry the equipment and complete the job.

Useful contacts

The Painting and Decorating Association (trade body):
www.paintingdecoratingassociation.co.uk
Training: www.coursesplus.co.uk

Landscape gardener

What is it?

There's far more to the job than the odd bit of weeding – at its simplest it involves garden makeovers, at its best it's something of an art form. It's a diverse industry and you can choose to specialise in different areas, including water features, building, paving, stonework, wind structures, decking, joinery, groundsmanship, draining and irrigation.

What's the appeal?

If you're definitely an indoors person who dislikes being open to the elements then it probably isn't for you. However, if you like getting your hands dirty, being creative, enjoy the outdoors and like to improve people's environments, it could be the job for you.

What skills do I need?

A comprehensive knowledge of plants and what can grow where is important, as well as good fitness levels. As the weather and other factors can hamper your work schedule, you need to be resourceful and plan carefully. To gain extra skills and knowledge, you could take a course at a horticultural college.

What does it cost?

It depends what level you wish to operate at but it is best to start small and hire any large equipment, such as cement mixers or cutting machines. It costs in the region of £25 a day to rent most pieces of equipment. You'll also need a van to transport equipment.

What can I earn?

Overhauling a garden – including clearing any rubbish – can earn you up to £100 a day, but you can charge more if the work involves design, creativity and sourcing materials, such as water features and stonework.

Any red tape?

You may find yourself handling pesticides, fertilisers and other chemicals and you'll need to use, transport and store these safely. There are also rules about wearing protective clothing when using certain machinery or equipment. Public liability insurance will cover you in the event of accidents.

Prospects for growth

According to the Horticultural Trade Association's figures, the landscape gardening industry employs over 60,000 people and has an annual turnover of approximately £3 billion – and it is growing.

Tips for success

You need to be prepared to get out there and sell your business. Much of the work you do will come from personal recommendations. People will ask their friends, their local garden centres or wholesalers to recommend someone reliable.

Pros

Gardening is not a seasonal job, confined to the summer – most of the work and planning are carried out in the winter months. Some landscaping, such as installing ponds or building walls can be done undercover in the event of bad weather.

Cons

Working outdoors can present difficulties if you are concentrating on soil work, as adverse weather conditions will prevent work being done. You might be confined to doing maintenance work in these times – or no work at all – so demand can come and go depending on the weather.

Useful contacts

Horticultural trade association: www.the-hta.org.uk
Directory of services: www.landscape-gardeners-directory.co.uk

Grass care

What is it?

Beautiful lawns may look easy to create but in reality they demand quite a bit of work. Being involved in grass and lawn care will include jobs such as watering, mowing, cutting, raking, fertilising and weed and moss control. You'll also be expected to analyse and spot potential problems or diseases that may affect the quality and growth of the grass.

What's the appeal?

It's suitable for those who enjoy fresh air, working in all types of weather and who like to use their hands.

What skills do I need?

No qualifications are necessary but doing a course will help to further your understanding of the factors that can affect grass, as well as helping you to spot any potential problems with customers' lawns before they take hold. You'll need to be physically fit too.

What does it cost?

Start-up costs are minimal – your customers should have most of the equipment necessary so you should invest in protective clothing and gloves. You might be required to carry out tasks that require specific tools, such as aeration and scarification, in which case you should hire these (around £11 and £40 respectively for a day's hire) and factor the cost of this into your fees.

What can I earn?

Rates will depend on location, the extent of the work you carry out and the size of the lawn. Pricing for treatments and a standard mow are around £15, whereas you can charge around £40 for more complex jobs that require specific tools, such as aeration and scarification.

Any red tape?

Handling pesticides, fertilisers and other chemicals needs to be done with care and attention. Observe health and safety rules when using lawn mowers and similar equipment.

Prospects for growth

Without proper grass care, lawns can deteriorate very quickly, so wherever there are gardens, there is likely to be work. Increase your appeal by taking pictures of other lawns you have looked after so customers are aware of your capabilities.

Tips for success

Spring is a good time to target customers – grass will need extra care after the winter months when the days get longer and the grass grows.

Pros

Contrary to what you might think, grass care isn't simply confined to the summer months, but can be carried out all year round, although demand is likely to be higher in the spring and summer months.

Cons

The work is physically hard and will involve a lot of bending, carrying and walking. You'll need to be prepared to work early in the morning but also finish late, at least in the summer months, to make up for shorter days in winter.

Useful contact

www.gardenadvice.co.uk

Lawn mowing

What is it?

The work involves mowing lawns but can also include hedge trimming, watering the lawn and grass cutting.

What's the appeal?

It's a job for those who love working outdoors and who enjoy tidying and working on conservation or environmental issues.

What skills do I need?

You'll need to be physically fit enough to deal with overgrown lawns as well as being aware of the environment around you, so you can spot anything in the grass that might prove hazardous when mowing.

What does it cost?

Most homeowners will provide you with a lawn mower so start-up costs can be minimal, or you can hire a rotary mower from around £15 a day. Safety is paramount when using either manual or electric lawnmowers, so you should ensure that you have sturdy boots as your feet are most at risk and wear goggles to protect your eyes from any flying debris.

What can I earn?

You could charge depending on the size of the lawn you are mowing or by the hour, where average rates are between £20 and £25. You'll need to factor exactly what the work requires – such as whether you will also be weeding and whether or not equipment is provided. You can charge more for other tasks such as hedge trimming and bagging leaves and grass.

Any red tape?

There are no specific regulations but safety is paramount when using lawn mowers so it's important to observe health and safety rules.

Prospects for growth

Mowing is one of the most important things that homeowners can do to maintain a beautiful-looking lawn, but few people have the time or inclination to do this. If you build up a good reputation and use word-of-mouth to promote your services, your lawn-mowing services can grow into more than just a part-time job. Consider offering other services such as weeding and raking so you can keep busy even when the grass is wet and not possible to mow.

Tips for success

Before starting to mow, have a good look around the garden to see if you can spot sticks, rocks and toys as these can all damage the mower. If you hit any of these objects suddenly, it can cause the mower to veer out of control, which could result in serious injury.

Pros

You can carry out lawn mowing at weekends so you can fit the business around other jobs.

Cons

Lawn mowing is very reliant on good weather as it cannot be carried out when the grass is wet so you may find the work limited to sunny days. You might also find yourself working at weekends and some lawn maintenance work will need to be carried out in the early morning or when the sun has set.

Useful contacts

Safety: www.safegardening.co.uk
Training and skills: www.lantra.co.uk

Tree surgeon

What is it?

Tree surgery involves the shortening of trunks, branches and limbs of trees, often to prevent excessive leaf drop, to allow views, to prevent branch breakage and to make the tree shorter and safer. Branches might also be dangerous or growing too close to a building.

What's the appeal?

It's a job suited to those who love working outdoors and who have an interest in the environment, trees and conservation.

What skills do I need?

Tree surgery is a very physically demanding job. It involves being outdoors in all weathers and using climbing skills. If you are operating chainsaws, you will need to have good practical abilities and you may also have to obtain a certificate or licence to use such tools.

What can I earn?

Wages initially can be low – starting at around £40 a day – but some tree surgeons earn between £150 and £200 a day, depending on the number of jobs undertaken and what they entail.

What does it cost?

Safety is important so you'll need equipment such as a hard hat, protective eyewear and leather gloves. Tools include lopping shears and saws – there are many different models and prices available, so personal preference comes into play. As a rough guide, lopping shears start from £30, but the more sturdy ones cost upwards of £100. A small chainsaw can cost from £170. You'll also need your own transport to carry the equipment.

Any red tape?

You need to take out public liability insurance as most customers are likely to check what insurance you have. Most tree surgery businesses have up to £5m cover.

Prospects for growth

Lopping trees is something that many people want to do but never get around to, or the tree is simply too high to reach, so the demands for this type of work can be regular. You could also consider offering other services to add value, such as tree pruning or crowning.

Tips for success

Some trees may be on the boundary of two properties, so it's a good idea to check that any neighbours are aware of the work you are carrying out. Tree surgery is generally a one-off job but reputation is important. Word of mouth will help promote your business so make sure you build up good relationships with your customers.

Pros

The work will help you to stay fit and you'll get plenty of fresh air.

Cons

The work can be dangerous, insurance costs are generally quite high and you need special equipment and skills to do the job safely and properly. Demand for the work will fluctuate with the seasons – you won't be able to carry out work in bad weather, such as thunderstorms and high winds.

Useful contacts

Arboricultural Association: www.trees.org.uk
Skills advice: www.lantra.co.uk
The Royal Forestry Society (tree management): www.rfs.org.uk

Garden maintenance

What is it?

Day-to-day tasks would typically include growing and taking care of plants, including weeding, pruning and watering, mowing grass, cutting away dead growth and generally tidying. Depending on the size and type of garden, you might also be expected to take care of ornamental spaces and features.

What's the appeal?

It suits someone who likes working with their hands, has an interest in horticulture and who enjoys fresh air.

What skills do I need?

No particular skills are required but it helps if you have an interest in plants and are able to recognise different species, especially types of weeds, and identify any potential diseases that may be affecting the plants and flowers. You'll need to be physically fit too.

What does it cost?

There are minimal costs involved as much of the equipment you may need can be provided by your customers. You should invest in clothing (overalls, gloves, protective glasses) and some basic gardening tools. You can always invest in new tools as the job demands, rather than buying equipment that you may not need up front.

What can I earn?

This depends on the type of work you are expected to do but rates of between £15 and £20 an hour are an average guide. If you have to buy any specific materials, such as pesticides, factor these costs in.

Any red tape?

If your job involves handling dangerous machinery, such as chainsaws or using chemicals and pesticides, you will need to have certificates of competence (available from awarding body NPTC). Be aware of the law pertaining to the use of hazardous materials, such as the Chemicals Regulations, Dangerous Substances and Preparations (Safety) Regulations, Control of Substances Hazardous to Health Regulations and the Health and Safety at Work Act. You'll also need public liability insurance to protect from any accidents.

Prospects for growth

Garden maintenance is one of those areas that most people know they should do more about but few want to, so demand can be high. Word of mouth is important for building new business in this line of work so ask your customers to recommend you.

Tips for success

If you have the necessary training and knowledge, you could enhance your skills beyond basic garden maintenance and offer advice on garden design and what to grow.

Pros

It's not a one-off job – if you build a good reputation, you could generate a reasonable amount of repeat business from a handful of clients.

Cons

It's physically demanding work, tough on the body and the hands as you will be bending, kneeling, carrying and lifting. Work is seasonal so expect to put in longer hours over the summer months, although gardens still need to be maintained during winter.

Useful contact

Training certificates: www.nptc.org.uk

Fencer

What is it?

Installing fences is one way to ensure privacy from neighbours and keep pets and children safe. Fences can be made from a variety of materials including wood, stone, brick, steel and other types of metal. Working as a fencer involves preparing the ground, measuring areas, calculating the amount of material needed and then building the fence. You might have to remove old fencing or clear any roots or weeds that are in the way as well as applying a coat of weatherproofing to the fence if necessary.

What's the appeal?

Fences can be decorative or functional or serve both purposes so the work is appealing to creative people, those who are good with their hands and those who are interested in safety aspects. You must also enjoy working outdoors.

What skills do I need?

You must be able to measure accurately and have a head for calculations as you will need to estimate how much material you will need for a given space. It's a good idea to be physically fit as the job can involve lifting heavy items or working with heavy pieces of machinery. You should also have a basic knowledge of construction and be able to use hand and power tools. As you'll be travelling to different sites, having your own transport can give you a head start.

What does it cost?

You'll need to invest in protective clothing and sturdy shoes, including ear protectors if you plan on using noisy equipment. You can hire the necessary tools from about £25 a day.

What can I earn?

Wages vary depending on region but fence erectors can expect to earn between £200 and £400 a week, and this can rise to almost £500.

Any red tape?

There are no specific regulations but you'll need to be aware of rules regarding health and safety and follow these carefully.

Prospects for growth

Fences are used in a variety of locations, such as homes and gardens, factories, sports grounds, farms and motorways so there are a good number of potential customers you can market the business to.

Tips for success

Think carefully about which type of fencing you want to specialise in, such as private homes or motorways and establish a reputation in this area first, before expanding to other types of fencing.

Pros

If you are prepared to work hard, you can earn a good income as a fencer, with minimal capital outlay.

Cons

You might have to work overtime and at weekends to complete jobs but you could try to charge more for working unsociable hours. Work is carried out in all weathers.

Useful contacts

Training and advice: Construction Skills: www.cskills.org; www.lantra.co.uk

Handyman/woman

What is it?

Home improvement and maintenance, involving all sorts of odd jobs around the home, including painting, plastering, putting up shelves, building cupboards and fixing windows and tiling floors.

What's the appeal?

It's a job for people who are good at fixing things and who get satisfaction from this. As the nature of the jobs varies, it's suitable for people with a range of background experience, such as construction, decorating, carpentry and electrics. Some of the work will also have a creative side to it, such as kitchen or bathroom fittings.

What skills do I need?

No formal qualifications are required but you will need to be good with your hands and it requires physical stamina as the work often involves prolonged standing, bending and working in cramped spaces. An interest in construction would also be helpful, including a good knowledge about how to fix parts of buildings that are broken and basic electrics. You should also be prepared to lift heavy objects. There are a number of courses available so you can continually develop your skills.

What does it cost?

You will need to purchase the necessary tools for the type of work you intend to carry out and ideally you should have a van or sizeable car to transport the equipment safely and easily. A basic kit will set you back around £50 but this will only have tools such as hammers, wrenches and a small hacksaw, so you'll need to invest in power tools such as hammer drills, which start from £100 upwards. Tiling tools, such as a tile cutter, costs around £40.

What can I earn?

You can choose to charge by the hour, the day or a flat rate per job done. Hourly rates tend to vary depending on the type of work you are doing and location but range from £30 to £80 and day rates can be up to £170. Consider how long it will take to complete the work, what skills you will be using and the type of materials required and factor these costs in.

Any red tape?

If you work in people's homes, you should get tradesman insurance, which includes public liability cover. You'll need to be up to speed with current health and safety rules too.

Prospects for growth

If you are prepared to work unsociable hours, you stand to earn a lot more as you can charge emergency callout rates.

Tips for success

The more skills you possess, the better. Ensure you have a basic toolbox. You may need specialised items from time to time but having a basic set of materials will get you started at a low cost and can cater for most home improvement tasks. Arriving on time will show reliability and mark you out from the rest.

Pros

It's a job that requires little education. Depending on your skills base, working as a handyman means you can be involved in a variety of jobs, creating a steady income from scratch.

Cons

You might have to work unsociable hours such as weekends and evenings, but you can consider charging more if you work at these times. There is strong competition in this job as start-up costs are low and it requires few qualifications.

Useful contacts

Training: www.constructiontrainingservices.co.uk
DIY advice: www.focusdiy.co.uk

Interior design

What is it?

You will plan and supervise the design and fitting of interiors and furnishings, giving advice and consulting at all stages of the process. The role could include space planning, checking work on-site, ensuring building regulations are respected and preparing drawings and documents relating to the design.

What's the appeal?

It's a very creative job and as each project is bespoke, tailored to a particular client's needs, no two jobs are the same.

What skills do I need?

A high level of design skill is essential, which would mean completing an interior design course or an art-based degree, although creative flair will also stand you in good stead. As you will be advising on colour schemes and fabrics, a visual eye is important as well as good communication skills as you will be liaising with clients and architects. Computer skills are also desirable, particularly computer-aided design (CAD) as you will be using a computer to develop sketches into more detailed drawings.

What does it cost?

An introductory interior design course starts from £650. Other than this, you will need a phone, computer and CAD software (prices start from £1,000 depending on your needs).

What can I earn?

Interior designers charge anything from £30 per hour upwards, according to the careers website Prospects.

Any red tape?

Professional indemnity insurance is a must to protect yourself against any claims for errors, omissions or professional neglect. You'll also need to be aware of building regulations pertaining to individual projects.

Prospects for growth

There are many trade shows for interior design, a useful hunting ground for contacts and networking. Check out the local builders and contractors in your area to see if they require interior design. You could consider specialising in offices, luxury homes, small spaces or country design. The British Interior Design Association offers members help with referrals for work, although you must have several years experience of the industry and have completed a recognised course in order to be eligible to join.

Tips for success

Prepare a portfolio of your design work to showcase to potential clients, this should include pictures of past interior design projects, with 'original' and 'after' shots, showing how you have transformed spaces. Interior design changes regularly so ensure you keep up to date with the latest trends.

Pros

The work can easily be carried out from your home, but will also involve a fair amount of time travelling visiting clients and sites so the role offers workspace variety.

Cons

Meeting deadlines are a big part of an interior designer's job, so you could find yourself working long and unsociable hours.

Useful contacts

British Interior Design Association: www.bida.org
Chartered Society of Designers: www.csd.org.uk

Wardrobe organiser

What is it?

It involves organising people's wardrobes and personal belongings, helping them to identify things they no longer need and enabling them to tidy up their possessions. It's also known as decluttering.

What's the appeal?

It's a job that can at times involve helping people who are experiencing a life changing moment, for example a divorce, bereavement or moving house. It's ideal for those who like being around other people, who like to listen and who enjoy making decisions and who like trying out new styles.

What skills do I need?

You should have an eye for fashion and know how to make the most of spaces. You should also be a natural when it comes to organisation and be happy dealing with people who might be resistant to change.

What does it cost?

There are minimal start-up costs involved. You will need to travel to people's houses and invest in some stationery which you can use to draw up examples of what you plan to do. It's also a good idea to take before and after pictures of other customers you have helped, and create some marketing material from this.

What can I earn?

You can expect to charge between £30 and £60 an hour, although prices will vary depending on size and location of the task. Remember to factor in travel costs as well.

Any red tape?

There are no particular regulations to be aware of, but you need to respect other people's homes and personal possessions. Ensure you set out any terms and conditions before starting any work.

Prospects for growth

This business will not make you a lot of money but it is something you can build into a fulfilling part-time business that can fit around other commitments.

Tips for success

Being a wardrobe organiser can be hard work, so ensure you are physically fit. If there are any issues you aren't prepared to tackle, such as cleaning, heavy lifting or removing items from the premises, make this clear from the start to avoid any misunderstandings later on. Ensure you set a time limit on particular projects so you can manage your and your client's expectations.

Pros

Decluttering someone's wardrobe can be very satisfying and it's about putting a natural skill to use. It's a useful source of top-up income.

Cons

People can often change their minds from one day to the next when choosing how to display clothes and what to get rid of, so it's important to be as flexible as possible.

Useful contacts

There is no formal training in the UK but you could choose to do a coaching course or one in interior design to help boost your existing skills.

Association of Professional Declutterers and Organisers UK: www.apdo-uk.co.uk

Upholsterer

What is it?

The work involves adding padding and soft covers to furniture, such as sofas, chairs and mattresses. Upholsterers can also be responsible for cutting and sewing and restoring antique furniture, they are known more commonly as craft upholsterers.

What's the appeal?

This job is suited to people with practical craft skills and those who take pride in their work. It can be carried out easily from home as you can set up an upholstery workshop in a spare room or garage for example.

What skills do I need?

You need to be good with your hands, creative and physically fit. You will also need to have patience as some of the work can be very delicate and will take time and attention to detail to complete. Some of the skills you need include hand and machine-sewing and the ability to work with different fabrics.

What can I earn?

Earnings vary but you can expect to get in the range of £210–£230 a week, rising to £340 a week, with those at the higher end making around £400 a week.

What does it cost?

Costs will vary depending on the type of upholstery you choose but much of the equipment you need can be found in a toolbox. For light upholstery work such as cushion covers and furniture needing lightweight fabrics, you'll need a sewing machine and they range from £200 to £1,500. You'll also need tools such as needles, pins, tacks, screwdrivers and awls as well as a foam cutter and staple gun.

Any red tape?

Materials used for filling furniture and mattresses must meet required standards of cleanliness and flammability. Upholstered furniture must pass a simulated test of a match or cigarette dropping on the furniture.

Prospects for growth

There is quite a high demand for upholstering antique furniture as it involves a certain degree of skill so your business can grow into quite a substantial one.

Tips for success

Decide what upholstery services you will offer so you can develop your expertise. You might want to focus on traditional upholstery, using materials such as horsehair or you might want to look at more modern techniques, using materials such as foam and polyester waddings. You can add value by offering a range of services such as curtain and loose cover making or sales of upholstery materials.

Pros

You can take on as few or as many projects as you want. It's a good source of extra income as you can work comfortably within your own home.

Cons

The work can be physically tiring as it is quite intensive and you might have to work long hours to get projects completed on time.

Useful contacts

Courses: www.cityandguilds.com

National Carpet Cleaners Association (NCCA), the trade body for upholstery cleaning: www.ncca.co.uk

Furniture repair

What is it?

Fixing broken pieces of furniture, restoring old furniture and minor upholstery repairs. It's something you can do within your own home, without the need to set up a workshop or splash out on expensive equipment. Some jobs can be carried out in your customers' homes, which would suit more expensive items that are difficult to move.

What's the appeal?

If you have artistic talent, furniture repair can be very satisfying. Although much of the work you carry out might be basic, you can put your creativity to good use with some refinishing touches. Fixing something that is broken can also be very enjoyable.

What skills do I need?

If you are patient and like to learn, you can carry out the majority of furniture repairs with basic skills. You will need to learn how to judge whether a broken piece of furniture can be fixed and is worth repairing – if the total cost is more than buying a replacement, then it doesn't make economical sense.

What does it cost?

You'll need a basic set of tools, many of which can be found in a toolbox or which can be bought for around £500. If you need any specialised tools or equipment, you could consider renting these to keep costs down.

What can I earn?

Charge per hour or per job done, but assess how many hours it may take you to carry out a particular job and don't forget to factor in the cost of materials and/or equipment.

Any red tape?

There are no specific regulations but as you might be dealing with expensive items or furniture that has sentimental value, you should protect yourself in the event of causing any damage.

Prospects for growth

This isn't a big money business but it can easily be built up into more than just a part-time job, particularly if you restore and repair expensive items.

Tips for success

Before restoring any type of furniture, you'll need to identify the type of material you are working with – this can often help you decide whether or not it's worth repairing. Ensure you work in an area that has plenty of light.

Pros

Being able to restore items of sentimental value can be immensely satisfying. Furniture repair is a good source of extra income and you can devote as much or as little time to it as you want.

Cons

You will need to be fit as much of the work may involve crouching or moving around in awkward positions. It can be physically tiring as it is quite intensive work.

Useful contacts

National organisation of craftsmen: The British Antique Furniture Restorers' Association: www.bafra.org.uk

Wallpaper hanger

What is it?

Applying wall covering and paper to decorate and protect walls, using materials such as paper, vinyl or fabric. The job will sometimes involve the removal of existing wallpaper, using methods such as steaming, soaking or applying solvents. You might also need to fill in wall cracks to hide imperfections that would otherwise show up through the paper.

What's the appeal?

This job is suited to people who are good with their hands, who are methodical, like attention to detail and who are creative. You'll also be consulting with people to help them design something they want, which can be satisfying and enjoyable.

What skills do I need?

You'll need to be reasonably fit as the job involves standing up for long periods of time. It helps to have a good eye for detail and colour and you'll also need to have an aptitude for calculations, as you'll be estimating sizes and quantities of paper.

What does it cost?

This varies, but basic tools are needed including pastes or adhesives, buckets, cloths and brushes. You'll also need measuring equipment so you should factor in around £500 to get started, but this could rise depending on the amount and type of equipment needed.

What can I earn?

Wages vary across the country and you can charge per job or per hour, rates are generally between £20 and £30 an hour. You'll need to assess the condition of walls, any work that needs to be done prior to papering, and any fixtures that might need to be removed and factor these into rates if necessary.

Any red tape?

There are no specific regulations but you need to be aware of any applicable health and safety rules.

Prospects for growth

There are many other ways to decorate walls, such as sponging, so the demand for wallpaper can come and go. It is also reliant on the strength of the housing market – if this is weak, people may put off building and redecorating.

Tips for success

Wallpaper hanging is a dying art but if you build up the necessary skills and experience, you could carve out a niche business with strong appeal. Practise in your home first so you can perfect your skills. Always order more paper than you think is necessary for a job as backup in case of any problems.

Pros

Most of the work is indoors so you will not be affected by adverse weather and no two walls will be the same, as they vary in terms of condition and shape. The business could grow and grow through word of mouth recommendations.

Cons

Work can be very exacting and repetitive, so you'll need to ensure you have plenty of patience.

Useful contact

Wallpaper Hangers Guild: www.wallpaperhangersguild.co.uk

House painting (interior)

What is it?

The work involves measuring surface areas of walls, stripping and cleaning them as well as filling in any cracks or holes in the walls. You might be carrying out a simple painting job or applying more complex finishes, depending on your levels of experience.

What's the appeal?

If you like the idea of transforming people's homes, have a flair for colour schemes, get a buzz out of physical work and enjoy methodical work then house painting could be the job for you.

What skills do I need?

You'll need to have an eye for measurements – as a painter you need to look at surfaces and calculate how much paint will be required. It's helpful to have a feel for colour and textures as you'll need to liaise with your customers on what types of paint would best suit their walls.

What does it cost?

House painting involves using a variety of tools, including steamers and paint spraying equipment. You can hire these from around £40 a day, though costs for more powerful spraying equipment start from £100 a day. You'll need a range of different-sized brushes and rollers which you can invest in and transport from job to job. You'll also need to invest in protective clothing, particularly masks and eyewear, as some paints and solvents can sometimes give off fumes, and a van to carry your equipment.

What can I earn?

For minor domestic jobs, such as painting a room, you can charge per job. This will take around two days to complete and average rates are between £150 and £300. For larger jobs consider charging a daily rate, which should take into account the amount of preparation, time and materials required.

Any red tape?

As you are likely to be using ladders and materials that emit fumes, ensure you have a good knowledge of health and safety rules. Cover up pieces of furniture carefully so you are not liable for any damage. Public liability insurance will protect your business from any damage to customers' property.

Prospects for growth

Most people hate painting and the thought of clambering up ladders and reaching awkward spaces so if you build up a good reputation, there could be plenty of opportunities to expand your customer base.

Tips for success

Think about specialising in certain types of interior painting, such as sponge-painting, to give your business an edge over the competition

Pros

House painting is a business you can start with minimal costs.

Cons

Painting involves long periods standing or bending in awkward positions, often on a ladder. You'll need to have patience and stamina and you may be required to work unsociable hours to meet deadlines.

Useful contacts

Construction skills: www.citb.org.uk
Trade association: Painting and decorating: www.paintingdecoratingassociation.co.uk

Property developer

What is it?

Fixing and renovating a house with the intention of selling or renting it.

What's the appeal?

For those who are keen on DIY, or want to escape their day job, renovating a house can help provide an outlet for creative urges.

What skills do I need?

It does not require any particular training or qualifications. Timing, however, plays a huge part and you need to be able to judge whether now is the right time for you. You also need to do the right research.

What does it cost?

A lot, and then some, so a good source of finance is vital. The costs in terms of time and money of maintaining, running and furnishing (if necessary) the property need to be taken into account. A management agency can help with this, but they will take up to 15% of your rent for the privilege.

What can I earn?

In the current economic climate investing in property no longer guarantees a great return, so check out how much other properties in your chosen area have sold for. If you have trouble selling, work out the rental yield, by dividing the annual rent by the purchase price.

Any red tape?

In September 2008, stamp duty was suspended for a year on houses costing less than £175,000. You will be charged 1% of the total value for properties of between £175,000 and £250,000, 3% for those between £250,000 and £500,000 and 4% for anything over £500,000.

Prospects for growth

Until you sell your first house, it's often impossible to grow or expand. In recent months, property values have plunged nationwide, so you'll need to do extra research if you are looking to invest in bricks and mortar. Check out which areas are still producing reasonable returns and be realistic about what these might be.

Tips for success

Being flexible about when you are able to view a property is crucial to getting the best deals. Think of your property as a product: who's going to be attracted to it, where do they want to be situated and what will they expect? Are you aiming to target first time buyers or retiring couples? Choose a property that is both suitable for sale and rental to maximise your opportunities.

Pros

The lack of any necessary overheads – as most of the work is done 'on site', you don't need office space. You can also fit the work around your existing job as it's possible to find a house, renovate it, and then sell it on at evenings or weekends.

Cons

There is still a genuine level of risk involved in property development and when things take a turn for the worst, there are very few ways to cut costs or reduce overheads.

Useful contacts

Independent property portal: www.homemove.co.uk
National Property Developers Association: www.npda.co.uk

House-sitter

What is it?

Taking care of a house, including paying bills, watering plants, tending gardens, picking up phone messages, looking after pets and perhaps cleaning, while the house owner is away. As a house-sitter, you agree to live in the homeowner's property for a given period of time or you provide a daily pop-in service.

What's the appeal?

It's a profession for people who like their own company and you have the freedom of choice to do as many or as few house-sits as you want. You can also house-sit abroad, helping to reduce travel costs. Many people house-sit in order to save money on living costs. It can also give you the opportunity to try out a new area you are thinking of moving to and to look after pets without the commitment or expense of owning them.

What skills do I need?

You need to be adaptable and respect people's homes and possessions. You should also be able to get on with people – although many house-sitters are on their own, you will need to build a rapport with the homeowner to match their requirements.

What can I earn?

House-sitters typically charge a fee of between £100 and £175 a week and you might also be able to charge travel fees on top if you are not physically staying in the house all the time.

What does it cost?

You will need to fund all your own day-to-day needs, such as food and drink and you generally agree to replace anything of the homeowner's that you consume. In some cases, you may be required to stump up a security fee to insure against any damage, which is generally the cost of a month's rent.

Any red tape?

There are no specific regulations, although if you register with house-sitting agencies to get your business started, you will need to fulfil their criteria and be prepared for background checks and is provide references.

Prospects for growth

This isn't a big money business, but you can develop regular house-sitting stints that fit in with your schedule and that work around your other jobs. Word of mouth and referrals is an excellent way of gaining new customers.

Tips for success

Ensure you agree who is responsible for costs such as bills before you enter into any agreement.

Pros

It can be a useful source of extra income and enable you to experience living in different areas.

Cons

If you don't like a particular arrangement, it can take time to sort out, particularly if the homeowner is based far away.

Useful contacts

There are a range of house-sitting agencies in the UK:

www.homesitters.co.uk

www.g-angels.co.uk

www.housecarers.com

Green home consultant

What is it?

Green home design considers the impact that buildings have on people and the environment. As a green home consultant, you will be assessing people's homes for levels of energy efficiency and advising them on how to improve these levels and be more environmentally friendly.

What's the appeal?

This job would suit someone who is environmentally conscious and who likes to offer advice to other people. Although you could run the business from home, the work would involve travelling and visiting other people's homes on a day-to-day basis and interacting with a number of other specialists.

What skills do I need?

The ability to listen, observe and project manage is important. You must also have a comprehensive knowledge of the latest developments in green products and materials, as well as any relevant legislation. For example since the end of 2008, whenever a domestic and commercial property is built or put up for sale or rent, it is necessary to have an Energy Performance Certificate that details how energy-efficient the building is. Courses are available in domestic energy assessment.

What does it cost?

There are virtually no start-up costs involved in terms of equipment needed, although you will need to invest in some marketing material to advertise your services. As you are likely to be travelling around, it helps to have a car. One that is eco-friendly is likely to create a good impression among customers. Alternatively, factor in the costs of public transport.

What can I earn?

The amount that consultants can earn varies enormously and the amount you will charge will be based on the type of job you are expected to do, how long it will take and how many people you will need to project manage or coordinate with.

Any red tape?

There are no particular regulations attached although you should be aware of health and safety rules when planning buildings work. Ensure you have a contract for all work carried out.

Prospects for growth

The concept of a green home consultant is a relatively new one, and is more widespread in the US than in the UK. It's a trend, however, that is catching on. Word of mouth is one of the best ways to generate business for consultants so ensure you get testimonials from customers.

Tips for success

Keep up to date with any legislative requirements and look at what other green projects are up and running around the country for inspiration.

Pros

Being a green home consultant is a good extra source of income that can be made as much or as little as you have time for. As you are likely to be working on different projects, there can be a fair degree of variety.

Cons

There's a fair amount of travel involved as you'll need to make a number of home visits for each project. This could be tiring depending on the locations you choose.

Useful contacts

Forum: www.buildingforafuture.co.uk
Information and advice: Centre for Alternative Technology: www.cat.org.uk

Declutter coach

What is it?

Helping hoarders to deal with their possessions, cleaning their homes in the process and even discovering the odd long-lost item or two. Declutter coaches, or declutterers, educate people on how to keep their homes tidy and help them to identify what things they need and what they can throw out.

What's the appeal?

You can help older people by making their homes more comfortable and reuniting them with lost possessions, or work with those who have recently undergone a life-changing personal experience, such as a bereavement or moving home.

What skills do I need?

Bags of patience and the ability to negotiate and be persuasive. Although many people will tell you they want to clear out their possessions, when it comes to actually doing so, they will be reluctant to part with the majority of it. Being tactful and objective is also helpful as much of the job involves providing moral support. On the practical side, you will need to have energy, be fit and have a good visual eye.

What does it cost?

There are minimal start-up costs involved as you will be travelling to people's houses and working in their homes. It's a good idea to take before and after pictures of other customers you have helped so new customers have an idea of the work you can do so invest in a digital camera.

What can I earn?

Average rates are between £20 and £30 an hour, with travel expenses on top, depending on the location and the complexity of the job.

Any red tape?

There are no particular regulations to be aware of, but you need to respect other people's homes and personal possessions. Professional indemnity insurance will help to reassure customers. Ensure you set out any terms and conditions before starting any work.

Prospects for growth

This business will not make you a lot of money but it is something you can build into a fulfilling part-time business that can fit round other commitments.

Tips for success

Offer a free initial consultation, so you can gauge exactly what the customer needs and how long it will take. If you have a car, you can offer to take away unwanted items to charity shops or to recycling tips within reason, to broaden your appeal.

Pros

Helping someone to help themselves can be immensely rewarding so working as a declutter coach can give you a real sense of satisfaction.

Cons

There is no real fixed pattern to the work – you might only be needed for half a day, or you might find yourself visiting one place once a week for a set period of time.

Useful contact

Association of Professional Declutterers and Organisers UK: www.apdo-uk.co.uk

Pool cleaner

What is it?

It involves cleaning and maintaining swimming pools, using products such as a sanitiser, a treatment agent that eliminates bacteria and other water contaminants, clearing leaves, checking water filters and pumps and ensuring water quality and temperature of the pool is safe for bathing. You may also be required to clean associated areas, such as spas and saunas.

What's the appeal?

It's a job suitable for those who like working with water, who enjoy cleaning and repair work and who like working with their hands.

What skills do I need?

You don't need any specific qualifications but cleanliness and organisation of pool areas must be kept to a high standard. A first aid qualification can be useful, together with a good awareness of safety issues. It's also useful to do courses covering the following: water sanitation and balancing, water testing, chemicals and filter and pump systems.

What does it cost?

If you work for individuals cleaning their pools, you'll need to provide your own cleaning materials, including leaf nets, chemicals, hoses, brushes, poles and automatic pool cleaners (similar to vacuum cleaners), which can amount to around £500. You'll also need glasses and gloves to protect your eyes and hands.

What can I earn?

Most pool cleaners charge by the hour, with rates of between £8 and £10. Factor in any travel costs on top of these and include any specific equipment you might need to buy over and above standard ones.

Any red tape?

Working with chemicals requires you to comply with acts such as the Chemicals Regulations, Dangerous Substances and Preparations (Safety) Regulations, Control of Substances Hazardous to Health Regulations and the Health and Safety at Work Act.

Prospects for growth

Most people know they need to clean their pools regularly but most don't want to, so demand for your services can be high.

Tips for success

Keeping a pool clean and free from pollution is not difficult – you need to test the water regularly to check for pH and chlorine levels. Most people use swimming pools in the summer so the work can be seasonal, meaning you can be very busy in the summer months with hardly any work in winter. Look to target those who have indoor pools so you can try and maintain some business over the winter months.

Pros

Much of the work will be outdoors so you'll get plenty of fresh air.

Cons

The nature of the job requires working some antisocial hours, such as evenings and early mornings as this is the best time to test water before adding chemicals, ensuring it's suitable for using that day.

Useful contact

Institute for Sport, Parks and Leisure: www.ispal.org.uk

Floral design

What is it?

Working with all types of flowers (cut, dried and artificial) and pot plants to design and make up floral arrangements for use as gifts and decorations. You could find yourself making up bouquets, advising customers on colour and flower types, setting up displays and making deliveries.

What's the appeal?

Being able to turn an idea into reality is very satisfying and you are involved in some of the most significant events in people's lives, such as weddings, anniversaries and birthdays.

What skills do I need?

Organisation skills and good timekeeping are a must – floral design involves working with delicate materials and delivering them on time for events. As many flowers are perishable, most orders cannot be completed too far in advance. Good communication skills are vital to ensure you can meet customers' requirements as is a good general knowledge of flowers, plants and the seasons.

What does it cost?

You'll need basic equipment such as scissors, knives, metal wire, paper and floral containers, such as pedestals and vases, as well as extra decorative touches such as tea lights. Many floral designers rent out workshop space so unless you can convert a garage, for example, you might need to consider renting some office/workshop space.

What can I earn?

This depends very much on what the client's requirements are, what type of flowers you are using and where you are based. Bridal bouquets for example start from £40, wreaths from £15, table centres from £15 and pedestals from £70. Ensure you factor in delivery costs on top.

Any red tape?

Do take out professional indemnity insurance cover to protect against any errors.

Prospects for growth

Floral design has low start-up costs and consequently there is a lot of competition, particularly around the summer months when weddings are likely to boost demand. Consider specialising in a particular market, such as weddings, and build up a portfolio in this area.

Tips for success

Training on the job is one of the quickest and best ways to make a career out of floral design, although it will almost certainly be poorly paid. You could also attend some courses in flower arranging to see if it is the right job for you.

Pros

This is a hands-on job and as you are working for different clients and events, tailoring bespoke designs, so there is plenty of variety. Many floral designers work with celebrities so there can be elements of glamour involved.

Cons

Early morning starts to source supplies from wholesalers are all part and parcel of the job – the earlier you go, the better choice you have, but you'll also have to work late nights at events. Your hands are also likely to need extra care and the job involves a lot of standing around.

Useful contact

Society of Floristry: www.societyoffloristry.org

Curtain maker

What is it?

Making curtains is not as simple as it might sound. Curtains are one of the largest expenses in interior decoration and involve accurate measurement, choosing and positioning curtain tracks and poles, calculating the amount and type of fabric needed, preparing estimates and hanging curtains.

What's the appeal?

This is a very traditional craft that still has a strong demand, particularly for bespoke curtains, so levels of creativity and job satisfaction can be high.

What skills do I need?

A good knowledge of soft furnishings and experience in hand finished curtains and blinds is valuable. You'll need to be able to use measuring tapes, sew and have a good eye for different types of fabrics and what type of curtain they are best suited to. There are many courses available covering these skills.

What does it cost?

A home study course lasting up to year can cost around £500. You'll also need to invest in a sewing machine (up to £2,500) and basic equipment such as measuring tapes, scissors and patterns.

What can I earn?

This varies depending on what type of curtains you are making, what materials you are using, where you are based and whether the curtains will be machine or hand-sewn. The cost of fabric should be added to any labour costs. Making curtains to order is generally more lucrative as the measuring, making and fitting of the curtains entails a considerable amount of work. The more complex the work, the more you can charge.

Any red tape?

Cover yourself with professional indemnity insurance to protect against any errors or neglect.

Prospects for growth

Consider whether you want to aim for the luxury or functional market or both. You'll be able to make more money and increase your business prospects if you stock fabric, but this will involve a greater investment in both money and space. Contact interior designers and soft furnishings providers in your area as they may be able to offer work.

Tips for success

Overestimating the amount of fabric needed may add to overall costs, but not having enough fabric to finish the job is an even worse scenario, so ensure you brief the client on the importance of having more rather than less material. Accurate measurement is an essential part of the job so ensure you are confident enough to do this properly.

Pros

This is an ideal business to run from home and one that is flexible (deadlines permitting) as you can work the hours you choose.

Cons

The work is quite painstaking and methodical, particularly if you are doing all the sourcing, measuring and sewing on your own, which could lead to problems with keeping up with demand. Take into account the time it will take to travel to people's homes.

Useful contact

Training: www.curtainacademy.co.uk

3

Health

Profile – Life coach
Who: Sue Atkins
What she does: Life coach
Where: Surrey
Set up business: 2005
Initial start-up costs: Substantial outlay

Sue Atkins launched Positive Parents in September 2005, a service offering parent coaching sessions to help improve parenting skills and build confidence and harmony within families, with the aim of inspiring parents to be the best they can be. One-day workshops are run throughout the year and one-on-one parent coaching is also available. Sue also sells parental advice products via her business' website, which includes toddler training and parent and teenager toolkits.

With a background as a teacher and a deputy head, it seemed natural for Sue to turn to coaching related to parenting skills. Qualifications have played a vital part in enhancing her learning and her business prospects. She is a qualified NLP (neuro-linguistic programming) Master Practitioner and has a diploma in life coaching from The Coaching Academy, one of the largest professional training schools in Europe. She is also a specialist in Thought Field Therapy, a technique for resolving parenting stress, anger and guilt and is listed on the International Register of Professional Coaches.

'Working on your own is quite a challenge when you have been used to working for someone else and having lots of chatty colleagues,' says Sue. 'You have to juggle all the hats from marketing and following up on leads, to changing light bulbs. You have to make room for all this as well as doing what you love which is the core reason why I started my own business.'

In Sue's words, it took 'a great deal of money' to set up the business as start-up costs included sourcing premises, setting up a website and investing in marketing. She also employed people to answer phones, used production facilities to record material and found a graphic designer to brand all her stationery and products as well as finding a publisher to produce them. She also spent a considerable amount of time and money networking to build relationships.

'There were expenses in terms of lunches and breakfasts and the provision of workshop facilities, but building a reputation in this field takes time and patience,' she says.

Learning about technology, search engine optimisation and return on investment has also been a learning curve. Sue believes it is important to have a really good web presence, as it provides ways to promote and up sell when you have done workshops. She invested £18,000 in the website and is still counting the costs.

'A website without investment in sophisticated search engine optimisation, tools such as Google AdSense, AdWords and pay-per-click is not worth doing – who is going find you?' says Sue. 'If you are setting up a website for your business, you need to work out who your market is, how global you want to be, and the levels of interaction you want online. Work out what marketing you need too.'

In terms of skills needed for coaching, passion is key to being a success, as is the ability to make a difference. Sue is now a regular speaker at events and workshops throughout the UK and is currently working on a series of bespoke coaching programmes for teachers, addressing issues of stress and preparation for Ofsted.

'Doing what I do is a huge privilege – you have the amazing feeling of having made a difference in someone else's life which can you give you a real sense of joy,' she says. 'Coaching also gives you the freedom to design your life, your day and your output and the job offers variety and the chance to meet interesting people.'

There are certain issues to be aware of if you are thinking of setting up a coaching business. Sue advises not to pack in your day job until you have a steady flow of clients. It's also a good idea to look for ways to market your expertise, such as being included in books and reports or by group coaching and helping to run workshops.

'You have to be extremely committed if not obsessive as it is a very difficult business to succeed in – people don't "get" what you do,' adds Sue. 'Take on board marketing advice and build a team of experts around you to support you.'

What one thing does Sue wish she'd known when she started? To promote a book she had written she hired a PR agency, but in retrospect she believes she should have given this more thought.

'I wouldn't have hired such an expensive PR agency on a contingency basis before looking into what it all entailed and meant. I could have had their advice for three months and achieved more,' she says. 'It's easy to make a lot of mistakes but really they are just learning experiences to pick yourself up from.'

Personal trainer

What is it?

There are various areas you can specialise in, such as helping people to lose weight, working with prenatal women or training athletes. As well as carrying out training sessions, you will work with clients to devise a personal training schedule for a set period of time.

What's the appeal?

It suits someone who likes to offer support as many clients will look upon you as a confidant. You'll also be keeping fit and have the opportunity to work outside of your home and outdoors.

What skills do I need?

There is no one UK exam which qualifies somebody to be a personal fitness trainer, but there are a number of courses that are well respected within the industry, and choice is determined by what area you choose to specialise in. Trustworthiness and reliability, being a good listener and the ability to relate to a lot of different people is almost as important as your skills as a fitness trainer.

What does it cost?

Other than the cost of training, which can be anything from £300 to £5,000, depending on what you specialise in and prior knowledge, other overheads are limited.

What can I earn?

The average hourly rate is between £20 and £50 and this very much depends on location and your skills.

Any red tape?

Public liability insurance is a must to cover you in the event of any accidents and will set you back around £100 a year.

Prospects for growth

Word-of-mouth is the most effective form of raising awareness and many personal trainers have also set up websites to give themselves a broader reach. As well as working with individuals, you could consider tapping into the corporate market, particularly those businesses that have in-house gyms.

Tips for success

Include a clause in your terms and conditions to protect you from people dropping out at the last minute or simply not paying. Or insist that people pay in advance for their sessions. If possible, undergo training in a range of fitness areas to keep your options open. Doing this will give you a good understanding of what you might want to specialise in. Update your knowledge of fitness techniques at least twice a year by attending courses run by recognised industry bodies.

Pros

There is a big target market – anyone who has found that diets don't work for them, for example, is a potential customer, as are those who like exercise but find it hard to motivate themselves.

Cons

While you can work as much or as little as you like because you are your own boss, the success of your business depends on you being available at times when it suits clients. This means early mornings, late nights and weekends.

Useful contacts

National Register of Personal Trainers: www.nrpt.co.uk
Training: www.ymcafit.org.uk
www.premierglobal.co.uk

Yoga instructor

What is it?

Teaching a form of stretching and exercise that aims to keep the mind, body and emotions in balance. It involves breathing exercises, attention to posture and meditation and aims to maintain fitness and muscle tone, aid with stress, energise the body and mind, and improve levels of concentration.

What's the appeal?

The tradition that is attached – yoga can trace its roots back more than 7,000 years and is a form of exercise that is steeped in heritage. There are also many different types so it appeals to someone who has the hunger to learn.

What skills do I need?

No academic qualifications are needed but you'll need to have experience of practising yoga with a qualified teacher, a recognised yoga teaching qualification and a good level of fitness. A first aid certificate is useful too, together with the ability to identify and meet pupils' requirements.

What does it cost?

Training can cost from £300 to £3,000. As far as equipment goes, you'll need a non-slip mat (£15–£30) and will need to rent out premises for classes, which could be a church hall, community centre, school or leisure centre. Membership of the Register of Exercise Professionals (£25) will enable you to show potential customers that you meet fitness industry standards of good practice.

What can I earn?

Hourly rates vary depending on location but are generally between £20 and £60.

Any red tape?

If you are considering offering yoga classes to children, you'll need to be checked by the Criminal Records Bureau. Make sure you have personal accident insurance (£46) and liability insurance (£46) and are aware of health and safety regulations.

Prospects for growth

Yoga is a popular form of exercise and as a yoga teacher you can work in a variety of places, such as sports and leisure centres, schools, health clubs and community centres. You could also consider tapping into the corporate market and targeting those businesses that have in-house gyms.

Tips for success

Target your classes at different levels of proficiency, such as beginner, intermediate and advanced, so you can widen your appeal. You could consider offering sessions of yoga comprising, for example, six lessons and ensuring that people pay up front so you can guarantee attendance.

Pros

You will keep physically fit and as most people come to several yoga classes, rather than one, you can build up a rapport with students.

Cons

Classes last between one and a half to two hours so they can be very intensive and physically draining and will involve working evenings and weekends.

Useful contacts

British Wheel of Yoga, the governing body for yoga in Great Britain: www.bwy.org.uk
Register of Exercise Professionals: www.exerciseregister.org

Pilates instructor

? What is it?

A form of exercise that focuses on building a body's core strength and improving posture, using low impact stretching and conditioning. It involves relaxation, breathing and repetitive movements.

✓ What's the appeal?

It can be done by anyone of any age and ability so you could be helping all types of people to improve their posture and body strength.

🔍 What skills do I need?

A background in exercise and attendance at regular Pilates classes – this is the first step to becoming an instructor. A recognised qualification is a must, as this will enable you to gain entry to the Register of Exercise Professionals, which will improve your chances of employment.

£ What does it cost?

A Pilates Diploma will set you back around £1,449. In terms of equipment, a mat will cost around £25, soft weights £10 and exercise balls around £4.50. You'll need an area to teach in, perhaps a room in your house but it will need to have enough space for people to stretch and move around and have a pleasant and relaxed atmosphere. Otherwise, you'll need to factor in the cost of renting space in a church hall or sports centre.

£££ What can I earn?

You'll be teaching in groups or giving one-to-one sessions, charging more for the latter. Fees vary depending on location and are generally around £20–£30 an hour although some instructors charge up to £60 an hour for private classes in London.

Any red tape?

Taking out public liability insurance is a must and you will also need a current certificate in CPR (resuscitation).

Prospects for growth

As a Pilates instructor, you can choose to work with individuals in their homes or at gyms and leisure centres. An increasing number of athletes and dancers are using Pilates to help recover from injuries, creating another potential market. Competition is fierce though so use word of mouth or consider building a website to promote your services.

Tips for success

Look for work on the internet, where there are many vacancies for Pilates instructors. The more flexible you are in terms of working hours, the higher the chances of finding work as most people will take classes in the evenings or at weekends. Look at specialising in pre or post-natal Pilates to broaden your appeal and attract new customers.

Pros

Pilates is a relaxing form of exercise so there is little stress involved in this line of work. Flexible work hours mean you can combine this with other jobs.

Cons

The role could involve a lot of travelling around to people's homes, which might reduce some of the hours you could work.

Useful contacts

The Register of Exercise Professionals: www.exerciseregister.org
Courses: www.futurefit.co.uk

Aerobics instructor

What is it?

Devising and leading group or individual exercise programmes, combining elements such as choreography, timing, music, balance and movement. You'll be demonstrating routines, showing people how to use equipment and expected to come up with varied routines tailored to different levels of fitness. You'll need to supervise participants to ensure they are carrying out routines properly and safely and be able to tailor routines for pregnant women or people suffering from lower back pain or weak joints.

What's the appeal?

It's a job suited to those who are in good shape, who enjoy structuring and teaching classes and who like to help people to improve their levels of fitness.

What skills do I need?

You'll need an outgoing personality and good levels of stamina and fitness, as well as the ability to lead, inspire and motivate people. Taking a course that leads to a recognised certification is essential, such as the Level 2 Certificate in Fitness Instructing, or you could start as an assistant instructor and complete work-based qualifications under the supervision of a qualified instructor.

What does it cost?

For courses, prices start from £1,200 and you will need to buy exercise clothes and a mat, and perhaps supply your own CD player if you intend to play music at classes. If you are working in a gym, they will supply the equipment for you and in other cases, you can combine aerobics with mat-based exercises and ask participants to bring their mats with them.

What can I earn?

Typically, you can expect to earn between £10 and £20 an hour.

Any red tape?

You need a responsible attitude to health and safety, a first aid qualification (including a resuscitation certificate) and public liability insurance. If you intend to work with children and vulnerable people you will need to show evidence of clearance from the Criminal Records Bureau.

Prospects for growth

There are various ways to build your business – you could work in gyms, health clubs or leisure centres or you could set up a class in community/school halls.

Tips for success

Check out the local gyms and fitness centres in your area to see what classes they run and when, and whether you can spot an opportunity to teach a type of aerobics class that they may not have on their schedule.

Pros

It will keep you in tip-top shape and there are a variety of courses you can do to improve your training and learn new skills.

Cons

It's not a business you can run from home so you must be prepared to travel and work evenings and weekends as you'll need to fit round other people's schedules.

Useful contacts

Training: www.premierglobal.co.uk

Register of Exercise Professionals: www.exerciseregister.org

Hairdresser

What is it?

This is a business that deals with the maintaining and styling of hair. Those that deal with male customers only are known as barbers. You could even choose to specialise in colourings. But there is also a vast array of other services on offer from hairdressers, including manicures and body piercings.

What's the appeal?

You don't have to rent expensive shop premises. Many businesses are mobile, where the hairdresser goes into customers' homes.

What skills do I need?

Before you even start to think about setting up, you should have several years' hairdressing experience of your own. Being a 'people person' helps as much of your business tends to be repeat visits from loyal customers.

What does it cost?

You'll need a certain amount of capital behind you if you intend to rent premises. For a mobile business, you'll need your own transport and equipment such as a pair of clippers (£60), colours, shampoos and styling products (£100) and good quality scissors (up to £200) and hairdryer (from £45). Other useful pieces include a set of heated rollers (£36), straighteners (£20) and a hand mirror (£3.95).

What can I earn?

Geographical location will affect your pricing. If you are based in the north of the country, a dry cut can cost upwards from £6, while in the south this could be upwards from £10.

Any red tape?

You may be using electrical items, from shavers and hairdryers to curling. Portable electrical equipment must be checked every two years to see that it is suitably maintained. One of the most important laws which hairdressers must abide by relates to hair dyes and shampoos, some of which can be hazardous. Care also needs to be taken in the handling of chemicals. Regulations known as Control of Substances Hazardous to Health (COSHH) have to be followed with regards to the use and storage of chemicals at work. You must also have public liability insurance.

Prospects for growth

There are many different types of hairdressing business which attract and cater for different sectors of the market. For example, there will be those that mainly have young urban professional customers on their books, those that attract families and those that attract the older generation. If you're running a female salon, bridal packages can be very profitable.

Tips for success

Always be passionate about learning and training as new practices and styles become popular.

Pros

It is a busy profession, particularly towards Christmas. It tends to inspire a great deal of loyalty from customers who will often visit the same branch for years.

Cons

Making mistakes with people's hair is not something they'll forgive easily. You could be cutting children's hair and many of the younger customers may well hate the experience of sitting in the chair swathed in a gown, so it's important to keep your cool in the face of any possible tantrums.

Useful contact

The Hairdressing and Beauty Suppliers Association: www.hbsa.uk.com

Beautician

What is it?

Offering facial and body treatments, concentrating mainly on the face, hands and feet, to improve people's appearances and help them to relax. Treatments can include facials, eyebrow shaping and trimming and the removal of unwanted hair. You may also branch out into applying and giving advice on make-up.

What's the appeal?

A passion for beauty – you will be helping to make people feel good about themselves as well as helping to transform their looks or getting them prepared for special occasions such as weddings.

What skills do I need?

A smart appearance and good personal hygiene are vital. You'll need to be able to communicate easily with your clients to find out what they want to achieve from the treatment and how they feel about their appearance. You should be friendly and approachable. You should have a qualification in beauty therapy.

What does it cost?

Course costs vary but as a guide, a beauty specialist course which includes most skills such as shaping eyebrows, facial massage, pedicure and manicure and make-up instruction will set you back £1,000. If you are setting up at home, you'll need a space that is comfortable, roomy and relaxing with seating – adjustable stools will set you back £50. If you choose to operate a mobile service, ideally you need your own transport. Investing in a salon will require considerable capital. Equipment wise, you'll need a uniform to protect your clothes (£25), a make-up kit (ranging from £30 to £250), facial treatments (from £3.00) and tweezers (£5.00).

What can I earn?

This varies according to the treatments you offer and where you are located, but most beauticians charge an average of £20 an hour.

Any red tape?

Get professional indemnity insurance and public liability cover. Your treatment area should be clean and all equipment sterilised. Any electrical equipment you use must be certified. If you join an organisation such as the Beauty Therapy Association, you'll need to abide by its code of conduct.

Prospects for growth

Widen your appeal and customer base by doing additional courses in areas such as ear piercing, waxing techniques, and epilation (hair removal).

Tips for success

Consider offering services such as massage, reflexology and aromatherapy to expand your skills base and widen your appeal. Ask customers about their medical history to establish if they have any particular allergies – you should carry out a thorough consultation before commencing any treatment.

Pros

You can work from home or travel to clients – the choice is yours, but the latter will give you more flexibility and the opportunity to widen your customer base.

Cons

There is quite a lot of admin involved as you will need to keep records of people's treatments and any reactions, particularly if you are generating repeat business.

Useful contacts

Hairdressing and Beauty Industry Authority: www.habia.org
Beauty Therapists Association: www.beauty.assoc.org.uk

Nail technician

What is it?

Improving the condition and appearance of people's nails by caring, repairing and sometimes extending them, using manicures for the hands and pedicures for the feet. You could also offer nail art services, which involves painting designs and putting transfers or small studs on nails.

What's the appeal?

It's a creative career and one that appeals to those who have a good sense of colour and who are interested in fashion and accessories.

What skills do I need?

Excellent hand-to-eye coordination is vital as well as good communication skills as you will need to understand your client's requirements and translate this into reality, as well as providing advice on aftercare. You'll need to have a good level of personal hygiene too. You can study to become a nail technician and a qualification will stand you in good stead with clients.

What does it cost?

A starter kit for nail technicians costs between £100 and £150, and you can add different items to this if necessary, such as nail art kits, which vary from a few pounds to £350 for a full airbush starter nail art kit.

What can I earn?

Prices vary depending on treatments. As a guide, you can charge £20 for a full set of nail extensions, £15 for nail art (charge more for using gems) and £20 for a manicure or pedicure.

Any red tape?

Health and safety is the most important aspect of this work – ensure you handle and store any varnishes and chemicals correctly and refer to the regulations on the

Control of Substances Hazardous to Health (COSHH). Use any equipment carefully and hygienically to avoid any possibility of damage or infection to clients' nails. You may need a license from your local environmental health department and ensure you have insurance to cover any treatments you give clients.

Prospects for growth

As well as travelling round to people's homes, you could consider offering your services to a range of other beauty-based businesses such as hairdressing salons, spas and specialist nail boutiques. You could try photographers and fashion designers too as they may need your services at photo shoots.

Tips for success

Nail art fashion changes regularly so ensure you keep up to date with the latest trends and techniques. You could consider training in other related areas to boost your skills base, such as skin painting and make-up. Train on friends and family first so you can perfect techniques and designs.

Pros

You can perform treatments in your own home although you are likely to generate more work if you travel to potential clients.

Cons

You might find yourself acting as a therapist too – when people are having their nails done, they often use the time to air any grievances.

Useful contacts

Hairdressing and Beauty Industry Authority: www.habia.org
Association of Nail Technicians: www.ant.uk.net

Life coach

What is it?

Life coaching helps people to gain more focus, direction and purpose in their lives. It can teach them to feel more confident, positive and optimistic and enables them to use existing skills better or to discover new ones. Coaching can also be aimed at specific areas, such as helping parents to bond with their children or helping people to better manage their time at work.

What's the appeal?

You will help potential clients to feel fulfilled in their personal and professional lives, so the job can be satisfying as you are helping them to achieve positive results. In terms of business coaching, you can help to raise levels of motivation and encourage people to look at their jobs in a new light.

What skills do I need?

There are no particular qualifications required although potential customers tend to look more favourably on those who have certificates and accreditations in coaching or a related discipline such as neuro-linguistic programming or teaching. Aside from training, good listening skills, an objective approach and the ability to motivate and inspire customers is essential.

What does it cost?

There are minimal start-up costs, such as travel to and from people's homes or workplaces and a laptop or computer to record sessions and organise admin. Expect to pay more to promote your business, investing in stationery and business cards and a website (which can cost from £500 to several thousand).

What can I earn?

According to Careers Advice, life coaches earn on average £50–£75 a session, although some can earn up to £250 an hour, particularly for corporate work.

Any red tape?

You will need to protect yourself with professional indemnity insurance and you may find it easier and cheaper to get cover if you are a member of a professional organisation.

Prospects for growth

As life coaching is not regulated in the UK, there is plenty of competition as anyone can become one. Clients can range from individuals to businesses and you could choose to specialise in certain areas to widen your appeal. Many leads are likely to come from networking and your reputation so it's important to gather testimonials from customers to boost referrals.

Tips for success

If you decide to do a course, choose one that is recommended by a professional body as this will help to boost your profile. To get your foot in the door for corporate coaching, consider offering a free consultation to businesses looking at areas such as motivation and staff morale.

Pros

The job is a good source of income and offers a high level of personal satisfaction. You'll be tailoring programmes to individual needs so there will be plenty of variety.

Cons

The work can be quite stressful at times as you could find yourself listening to a range of emotional issues and problems.

Useful contacts

www.coachingnetwork.org.uk
www.coachfederation.org.uk
www.associationforcoaching.com

Marriage counsellor

What is it?

Many married couples experience difficulties at some point in their relationship. A marriage counsellor does not give advice but provides a way for couples to communicate with each other in a constructive way, by understanding and confronting any underlying issues that may be causing problems.

What's the appeal?

The experience of helping people to address or resolve a difficult situation can be extremely rewarding – working as a marriage counsellor puts a tremendous amount of trust and responsibility on your shoulders so you must be comfortable in these sorts of situations.

What skills do I need?

There are no set academic qualifications but many people approach the profession with a background in psychology, education or a health-related subject. A pre-entry qualification is vital, such as a course accredited by the British Association for Counselling and Psychotherapy (BACP), which will enable you to practise counselling in a wide variety of settings or a part-time course in counselling. On the practical side, you will need to be patient, be able to listen, be objective and have empathy as well as an appreciation of confidentiality issues.

What does it cost?

Part-time introductory courses from an adult education centre cost between £100 and £300. It's a good idea to carry out counselling sessions in a neutral space, so if appropriate, you could use your premises or you may have to rent a space.

What can I earn?

Private marriage counsellors charge between £20 and £50 an hour, the optimum length of time for sessions.

Any red tape?

There are no formal legal regulations but there are standards to adhere to if you want to be accredited by the BACP, for example, which will help boost your profile in the eyes of potential clients.

Prospects for growth

As well as working privately, you could consider offering your services to local GP practices.

Tips for success

Consider offering your services on a voluntary basis to start with so you can ascertain whether this is the right role for you, pick up some advice and build useful contacts. Gather as much background information as possible on potential customers so you can tailor sessions to their needs.

Pros

Phone and internet counselling is on the rise so you could find that much of the business can be carried out from home.

Cons

Length of work can vary enormously – some people will only need a few sessions whereas others can take months to work through their problems, so you are never quite sure how much or little work you will have. The job can be stressful and intense because of the nature of the subject matter and the fact that you will often be working in small groups.

Useful contact

BACP: www.bacp.co.uk

Companion for elderly person

What is it?

Looking after the needs of elderly people, which could involve undertaking errands and shopping, preparing meals, light cleaning, helping them to bathe and dress, and accompanying them on short walks or driving them to hospital appointments. You might be required to look after people with specific needs, such as those who are disabled, recovering from a stroke or with Alzheimer's.

What's the appeal?

You will be helping vulnerable and frail people to gain independence as well as providing them with a source of companionship and enabling them to enjoy days out.

What skills do I need?

There are no specific qualifications but many companions have done some training as carers. It's more important to be compassionate, trustworthy, punctual, patient and have a reasonable level of fitness, as well as having the ability to get on with people. A first aid qualification is useful too.

What does it cost?

You'll generally only need to factor in your travel costs, which should be minimal as the role suits people who are local to the elderly person so they can be reached quickly if necessary. All other expenses should be paid for by the customer so ensure these are factored into your earnings.

What can I earn?

Rates vary depending on location and duties but as a guide you can expect to get between £10 and £15 an hour.

Any red tape?

There are no specific regulations but any potential customers are likely to want to see a Criminal Records Bureau (police) check and at least two character references.

Prospects for growth

This type of work won't earn you a lot of money but as many companions are required for between one to four hours a day, it is possible to take on a number of clients in one week and still have time for other commitments. You can find a number of vacancies online or through classified ads, as well as advertising your services in local libraries or church halls.

Tips for success

Ensure you know exactly what duties you will be required to take on and any relevant medical history so you can be as prepared as possible in the event of any emergencies. If you want to become a companion for elderly people with specific needs, it is a good idea to undertake an additional qualification in caring for such people.

Pros

The work is normally very local so you won't have to travel far and being able to help someone who may not be able to help themselves can be very rewarding.

Cons

The work can be lonely and physically demanding, depending on the needs of the person you are looking after.

Useful contact

United Kingdom Homecare Association: www.ukhca.co.uk

Nutrition specialist

What is it?

Giving advice to people on what and what not to eat. You will be planning food and nutrition programmes, making diet plans and advising on the preparation of meals. The role also involves raising awareness of healthy eating and you could be giving advice on cooking and shopping for healthy food.

What's the appeal?

If you enjoy learning about food and how to improve people's well-being, then working as a nutrition specialist can offer a high level of job satisfaction.

What skills do I need?

If you want to practice as a nutrition specialist, you'll need a qualification, such as the Nutrition Specialist Diploma, and you don't need any experience to start the diploma. It is endorsed by The Nutrition Society, the largest society for nutrition in Europe. Alongside a good knowledge of the importance of a good, balanced diet, you will need the ability to inspire and motivate people. Good communications skills are a must as you will be liaising with clients, listening to their issues and offering advice on nutrition.

What does it cost?

Apart from training costs (which start from £1200), there are minimal start-up costs. You can visit potential clients in their own home, or if you choose to offer your services to public health organisations, for example, you can rent office space on their premises.

What can I earn?

You can earn between £20 and £40 an hour on a one-to-one basis or up to £80 an hour working with small groups.

Any red tape?

You must be insured with professional indemnity insurance. If you join the register of The Nutrition Society, you'll need to abide by their code of conduct.

Prospects for growth

Obesity levels are on the rise and people are becoming increasingly conscious of the need to eat healthier foods and to have a balanced diet. Getting work can be a challenge though so look to offer your services to a related industry, such as a personal trainer, or even consider doing a personal training course that combines nutritional aspects. To succeed in this business, the more qualifications you have, the better.

Tips for success

Nutrition is an area that is under constant development so it's important to keep up to date with new research by undertaking regular courses.

Pros

The job offers plenty of variety as you will be working with people who have different needs and who will require different treatments.

Cons

Competition is fierce and there is quite a lot of administration involved as you need to keep records of consultations and detailed case notes.

Useful contacts

British Nutrition Foundation: www.nutrition.org.uk
www.nutritionsociety.org

Masseuse/masseur

What is it?

You'll be massaging customers through structured pressure and tension, applying oils to their skin to relieve tension, help them relax or to deal with painful areas. You could choose to specialise in certain areas, such as sports massage to help treat injuries, prenatal massage, Thai massage, deep massage, and baby massage, helping parents to bond with and calm babies. You might also find yourself giving advice to clients on additional exercises they can do to relieve pain and promote muscle flexibility.

What's the appeal?

Helping people to overcome pain and pressure points, as well as advising them on simple exercises to help combat future muscle problems.

What skills do I need?

There are no particular qualifications required but the General Council for Massage Therapy (GCMT) recommends taking a course before beginning work. You'll need to be confident working closely with clients, look smart and have good personal hygiene. Good communication is essential for effective massage as you'll need to assess the client's requirements in order to offer the best service.

What does it cost?

You'll need a massage table (from £159), covers (£8.99), couch rolls (£25), oils (around £3.50 each) and plenty of towels. You can clear a room in your home but ensure you have enough space as a cramped area will not convey the right atmosphere.

What can I earn?

Hourly rates vary depending on the type of massage but as a general guide, look to charge between £20 and £60 an hour.

Any red tape?

At present, massage therapy is an unregulated area. If you want to go on the register of the GCMT, you'll need to abide by their rules of conduct and produce certificates and evidence of insurance. Ensure you cover yourself with professional indemnity insurance and be aware of the Health and Safety Act.

Prospects for growth

Consider offering different types of massage so you can broaden your appeal. People usually seek a massage therapist for the treatment of pain caused by poor posture, accidents or sports injuries so you could contact your local gyms and doctor practices for potential referrals. Recommendations from satisfied customers are important in this line of work.

Tips for success

Being a mobile massage therapist is more flexible and will give you access to a wider customer base, but you will have to carry your equipment with you so you'll benefit from having a car, which will incur more expense.

Pros

You can work as many or as few hours as you choose and as customers have individual needs, the work can be quite varied.

Cons

There is a lot of competition in massage from other therapists, including osteopaths, physiotherapists and those who practise complementary medicine.

Useful contacts

General Council for Massage Therapy: www.gcmt.org.uk
Training: www.massagetraining.co.uk

Physiotherapist

What is it?

You will be treating physical problems caused by illness, accident, injuries or ageing, working with people of all ages and using your hands or electrical machines. You could also be advising patients on how to prevent future injuries and drawing up exercise plans.

What's the appeal?

You will be helping people to make positive changes to their health and bodies and can work with a diverse range of people, from children to the elderly. You can carry out treatments in your home or visit those of patients.

What skills do I need?

In terms of qualifications, you would need to complete a course of study – the majority of physiotherapy programmes comprise of three to four years of study but there are other options, such as longer, part-time programmes that are work-based (so you could work as a physiotherapy assistant and learn on the job) and accelerated two-year programmes for those in a related discipline. Patience and compassion are important as you will need to help identify where people are experiencing pain and work out the best way to treat it. You must be able to empathise with patients.

What does it cost?

Physiotherapists use a range of equipment such as couches (£200–£279), gym balls (£25) and joint support belts (£16.95). If you can't use your home for treatments, you'll need to consider renting a space in a GP's office, health centre or sports club.

What can I earn?

Earnings vary considerably – some physiotherapists can earn up to £150 an hour, but average rates are between £30 and £50 per session, with higher fees if you choose to make home visits.

Any red tape?

You will need professional indemnity insurance. In order to become a chartered physiotherapist, you need to do a degree approved by the Health Professions Council, which will mean you are eligible for membership of the Chartered Society of Physiotherapists.

Prospects for growth

You can choose to specialise in certain areas to broaden your appeal and increase your learning. Many physiotherapists start out by offering services to GP practices, so this is an avenue to explore to build up contacts. The stronger your qualifications and work experience, the better your chance of building the business.

Tips for success

Physiotherapy is a profession that benefits from continuous learning so you should be eager to undertake courses in order to improve your knowledge and your services.

Pros

It offers academic and physical challenges and there are numerous areas you can specialise in, such as patients with sport injuries, the elderly or those with learning disabilities.

Cons

The competition – physiotherapy courses have more applicants per place than nearly any other degree subject in the UK.

Useful contact

Chartered Society of Physiotherapy: www.csp.org.uk

Chiropractor

What is it?

You will be diagnosing and treating problems related to joints, bones and muscles and the effects these have on the nervous system, with a particular focus on the spine. Chiropractors use their hands to manipulate and make gentle adjustments to improve the efficiency of the nervous system, working with areas such as the neck, back and legs.

What's the appeal?

You'll be helping those who are experiencing pain or discomfort as the result of illness, injury, poor posture and lack of exercise. From a personal level, the job can be very satisfying.

What skills do I need?

A degree – entry requirements for this vary but usually involve academic qualifications in science-based subjects. If you have paid or voluntary experience in a caring role, this may stand you in good stead. The ability to give clear advice and communication skills are vital as treatments start with a consultation, involving a detailed discussion of the patient's symptoms and what you can do to help. You need to be able to instil a sense of trust and empathy with the patient.

What does it cost?

You'll need specialist equipment, such as a treatment couch (prices vary but can cost up to £2,000), a chair and tables for consultations and a changing screen (up to £180). You can use a room in your house or rent out space so factor this into costs.

What can I earn?

The majority of chiropractors are self-employed with typical earnings ranging from £25 to £60 an hour. Charge on the higher side if you are travelling to people's homes.

Any red tape?

You need to be registered with the industry regulator, the General Chiropractic Council (GCC) before you can practise as a chiropractor, and to join the register, you need to have completed a GCC-accredited course. If you want to join an organisation such as the British Chiropractic Association, you need to spend a year working under the supervision of an experienced and qualified chiropractor, or you could work as an associate chiropractor within an existing practice or have supervised sessions whilst working on a self-employed basis. Ensure you have professional indemnity insurance.

Prospects for growth

According to the British Chiropractic Association, the profession is growing year on year. Some patients are referred by GPs, so establish links with local surgeries. Many people self refer so it's important to build up a good reputation.

Tips for success

Ensure you keep your skills and training up to date and consider specialising in certain areas such as sports injuries. Registration with the GCC is also dependent on doing at least 30 hours continuing professional development every year.

Pros

You can find yourself working with a variety of people in a variety of locations, such as their homes, health clinics or outdoor at sporting events, so the work is diverse.

Cons

The work can be physically demanding as you will be on your feet for most of the time and you will need good upper body strength. It can take time to build up a practice and establish clients.

Useful contacts

British Chiropractic Association: www.chiropractic-uk.co.uk
General Chiropractic Council: www.gcc-uk.org

Osteopath

What is it?

You will be treating a wide range of patients and conditions that usually arise from accidents, sports injuries, work strains, poor posture and diet. Treatment involves gentle, manual techniques to help ease pain, reduce swelling and improve mobility. It does not involve any use of drugs.

What's the appeal?

You could and yourself working with a wide range of people, from the elderly to children and babies, and women going through posture changes caused by pregnancy. As each condition is different, there is a wide range of variety in this role.

What skills do I need?

Training is both demanding and lengthy and you would need to complete an accredited degree and be registered with the General Osteopathic Council (GOsC). If you are already medically qualified, a shorter programme may be an option. An interest or previous exams in science and medicine are usually required, alongside people skills such as the ability to listen, reassure, empathise and be tactful. You'll need to have good observational skills to determine what the best treatment is and to be able to communicate this clearly to the patient.

What does it cost?

Treatment rooms have bare essentials. You will need a suitably sized space (a room that is no less than 9' by 7'), a treatment couch (£200–£300) and a desk and chairs for consultations. You could consider renting a space in a GP's office.

What can I earn?

Typically, you can look to charge between £25 and £50 for a 30–40 minute session, according to the GOsC.

Any red tape?

By law, you need to be registered with the GOsC, have completed a course of training that is accredited by the GOsC and provide evidence of public liability insurance as well as character references. Ensure you have professional indemnity insurance.

Prospects for growth

According to the GOsC, osteopaths carry out around seven million consultations a year, reflecting an increase in demand over the years. The vast majority of people who visit osteopaths self refer so it is important to build up a good reputation to increase your profile.

Tips for success

Consider shadowing an osteopath at work to see if it is the right move for you as training is not to be entered lightly. If you don't have any science qualifications, you can complete an Access course to help get your science knowledge to the right level.

Pros

You can choose the hours you want to do and still earn a steady income and helping people to overcome pain can be very satisfying.

Cons

Training is intense so osteopathy is not for those who shy away from courses and learning. As you will be lifting people and sometimes using positions that are not natural, the work can be physically tiring.

Useful contacts

GOsC: www.osteopathy.org.uk

4

Children

Profile – Baby and children's products online

Who: Holly Wright

What she does: Personalised books for babies and children

Where: Somerset

Set up business: 2004

Initial start-up costs: her start up capital was £60,000 (from remortgage) and she started paying herself a salary in year three (she earned money freelancing as a writer in the meantime).

It's Your Story.co.uk, set up by Holly Wright in 2004, is an internet business specialising in personalised books, cards and party invitations for children and babies. The child or baby's face is incorporated into the illustrations and their name and other information about them is included in stories.

The idea for the business was inspired by Holly's parents, who decided to make personal storybooks for their growing number of grandchildren. At the time, Holly was working full time as the editor of a trade magazine focusing on marketing issues.

'My father took photographs of my long-suffering mother in various poses, such as hiding under the table and crouching amid the flower pots, and they wove it into a story called "*Where's Granny?*",' says Holly. 'The grandchildren were bowled over by the idea as their grandmother featured in the pictures as well as in the story.'

Although there were a number of personalised story-books on the market where the child's name was included in the story, nobody had taken the next step of personalising the illustrations.

'I had worked for my employer at the time for nine years, climbing the ranks since leaving university,' explains Holly. 'I knew about the publishing world, and realised that the advent of digital print and digital cameras made this next level of personalisation possible.'

One conversation with her future husband about her idea and his immediate response of 'go for it' was all Holly needed to follow the courage of her convictions that the idea would work. Six months later she had handed in her notice, remortgaged her flat to raise the necessary capital, found two illustrators and struck up a partnership with a digital printer and website design company.

Day-to-day, Holly is involved in everything from processing orders and dealing with customers to paying invoices, doing the company's VAT return, meeting with suppliers, developing new products and brainstorming ideas.

'I also field calls from people who want to sell advertising, update the website with the latest feedback, check our Google ranking and tweak it,' adds Holly. 'I am obsessive about our site statistics, such as who's visiting the website.'

She says a high level of self-motivation is also essential as well as the ability to be flexible and resilient – everything falls to her from the mundane, repetitive tasks such as downloading images from the site to putting together business proposals and financial forecasts.

'Inevitably, there are also a lot of knock backs you need to be able to deal with – this can be anything from a major piece of PR coverage not coming off to a third-party tie up falling at the last hurdle when you've already invested significantly in the partnership,' she says.

The most daunting part of setting up the business was leaving the security of a full-time job – particularly, Holly says, when it involved taking precious equity out of her property. This fear factor never entirely disappears, particularly in the current economic climate.

'There's no team around to bounce ideas off or to share the highs and lows of the business,' she says. 'But one of the best aspects of the work is the huge buzz I get when something does come off. Nothing beats the high of business success when it's your own company and purely down to your own graft.'

Holly is also now in a position where she is taking a salary out of the business and it is turning a profit.

'It's not a big salary or a big profit, but we have invested significantly in the last two years in new products and website development so this is quite an achievement,' she says.

Her advice for budding entrepreneurs? Before getting caught up in the brilliance of your idea, spend serious time working out how you are going to tell people about it – in her opinion, the idea is the easy bit.

Childcare

? What is it?

Childcare or childminding involves looking after and caring for babies and children up to teenagers, in return for payment. You will be offering playtime, learning opportunities, trips to the park and other activities, as well as one-to-one attention. You will also be expected to provide meals.

✓ What's the appeal?

The chance to work flexible hours in your own home, so you can combine caring for your own children at the same time, although some childminders work in the child's home.

🔍 What skills do I need?

Patience, enthusiasm and the ability to take responsibilities seriously while maintaining a sense of fun. No qualifications are necessary but taking childminding and first aid courses will improve your chances of success.

£ What does it cost?

There are minimal start-up costs as you can run the business from your own home, using existing facilities, although you'll need to ensure your home is safe and child friendly.

£££ What can I earn?

Childminders set their own fees so ask your local authority what the rates are in your area. How much you earn will depend on location, the number of children you look after and the hours you work. According to the Daycare Trust, the typical cost of a full-time place with a childminder for a child under two in England is £144 a week, £139 a week in Scotland, and £153 a week in Wales.

Any red tape?

All childminders that intend to care for children under the age of eight for more than two hours a day have to be registered by Ofsted, the Office for Fair Standards in Education. An inspector will visit your home to make sure you are suitable to care for children and that your home is safe and child friendly. You'll need to pay a registration fee and public liability insurance is also a must.

Prospects for growth

Childminders are in demand and work can build steadily through word-of-mouth. There is plenty of government support and as a newly registered childminder you might be eligible for a grant to cover set-up costs, available from your local authority.

Tips for success

Local authorities hold preregistration briefing sessions where you can learn more about being a childminder and whether it's the right job for you. Get in touch with experienced childminders as they can offer you help and guidance.

Pros

You can meet and network with other childminders in your area and become part of the local community.

Cons

The income from childminding is not huge and can be unreliable and your belongings and home will suffer from wear and tear.

Useful contacts

Your local authority
Advice on careers: www.childcarecareers.gov.uk
National Childminding Association: www.ncma.org.uk

Children's clothes online

What is it?

Selling children's clothes via the web. It is easier to buy these online than adult clothes as most parents don't normally need to try children's clothes before they buy, especially in the case of babies and small children.

What's the appeal?

This business can be run easily from home at hours to suit you. The beauty of an online business is that it is just about suited to anyone and you can start the business from anywhere, as long as you've got access to an internet connection.

What skills do I need?

For any online business, you will need to have good organisational skills as you will be dealing with a variety of tasks at the same time, such as web design, selling, delivery, marketing and sourcing products. You don't need to be technically minded but it helps if you have a good idea of what you want your site to do before you embark on the build and design.

What does it cost?

The cost of setting up a website varies enormously – from £500 for a basic one to £2,000 plus for a site with more applications. The key is to start off small and then add features and functionality as you go along and according to demand.

What can I earn?

This depends very much on the products you will be selling, what price you can buy the stock for and what mark-up you can achieve on sale.

Any red tape?

Any business that sells online needs to comply with the Distance Selling Regulations. You'll also need to clearly display your contact details on your website.

Prospects for growth

Start off small and work on the site part time before you decide whether to commit to it. Some online businesses have taken off in a very short space of time, while others have not. You need to invest a certain amount of effort to get your business noticed when it's solely based online, such as using search engine optimisation and pay-per-click advertising but this all takes time to make an impact.

Tips for success

Do your research carefully – can you spot a gap or niche in the market? Don't invest in too much stock until you can gauge demand.

Pros

It's a good part-time option for working mothers as you are likely to have a good idea of the types of products that appeal and can do as many or as few hours as you want.

Cons

There is a lot of competition in this area so you will need to invest time and money in your marketing and your website to stand out from the crowd.

Useful contacts

Advice on regulations: www.oft.gov.uk
www.businesslink.gov.uk

Baby products online

What is it?

Selling baby clothes, products and equipment via the internet. Customers buy directly from your site and the products are delivered. You will need to display pictures of the products and offer customers the ability to buy online, by either having a transactional facility built on your website or a phone number they can call to place their order.

What's the appeal?

It's a business that can be easily run from home so you can fit this around childcare and other commitments.

What skills do I need?

You need to know about your products – clothes in particular come in and out of fashion quickly so ensure you are up to speed with the latest trends in baby clothes. You will also be dealing with the public on a regular basis, so will need to have good communication skills. Sourcing from suppliers requires the ability to negotiate.

What does it cost?

The cost of a website varies greatly – from around £500 for a basic one to £2,000 for a more sophisticated one to five times that if you want added functionality. Decide how many pages you want and the necessary content. You can always go back and add new pages. The amount you spend on your stock depends entirely on what brands you want to sell, such as low-end or more upmarket ones.

What can I earn?

This really depends on what products you are selling. Maintaining a website is not costly, but in the early stages on any money made is likely to be reinvested in marketing. Don't expect to become an online millionaire overnight.

Any red tape?

Selling items over the internet, phone, by mail order or digital TV requires you to comply with the Consumer Protection (Distance Selling) Regulations. You must display certain information on your website, such as your business name, physical address and email address.

Prospects for growth

One of the keys to raising the profile of your website is to make it more search engine friendly by working out what the best keywords would be – the words that someone would type into a search engine if they were looking for a website like yours.

Tips for success

Start off with one category before moving onto others, depending on demand. Selling baby clothes is one of the most popular areas as babies tend to grow out of these very quickly so demand is high. If building your own website is not an option, try searching for web designers online, or ask friends for any recommendations. Consider partnering with other websites to sell and advertise your products.

Pros

This is a work-at-home business and depending on how big you want the business to grow, it requires a few hours a day, updating items that are sold and adding new inventory. You can start off small and work on the business part time before you decide to commit to it.

Cons

It can take time for an internet business to grow, particularly one targeting baby products as the market is extremely competitive.

Useful contact

Legal information: www.oft.gov.uk

Baby and child products party seller

What is it?

It involves selling products for mothers and children from birth to age five. This type of company is more common at present in the US than in the UK, and generally involves signing up to a baby and child products home party seller, acting as consultant and selling the products in your own or other people's homes to a group of invited people.

What's the appeal?

It's a good opportunity to make money while having fun and meeting new people. You can either host baby and child product parties in your own home or travel to others – people often feel more inclined to buy products in their own homes.

What skills do I need?

Motivation and convincing demonstration and sales techniques as you will have to describe the product to people face-to-face. To sell via this medium, you have to have products that are useful so you need to be able to convey this.

What does it cost?

The easiest way is to sign up as a consultant to a baby and child products party seller and buy one of their starter kits – in the US, prices for this range from £50 to £200. You could choose to source your own products but this will take time and cost you more.

What can I earn?

This depends very much on what type of products you are selling and at what price and whether you are aiming for a luxury or more budget-conscious market.

Any red tape?

If you are selling face-to-face in someone's home or place of work, you will need to abide by the Doorstep Selling regulations.

Prospects for growth

Marketing the business successfully is the key to getting bookings. Target mums-to-be and those with young children by advertising your services at playgroups.

Tips for success

If you're buying into a party selling business and acting as consultant, check out what you get for the initial fee, such as what's included in the starter kit. Look for samples and training materials as these will help you when it comes to hosting the party – your products should have an edge over what is already easily available. Make sure there is a demand for the products and test your approach on friends and family first. Always invite more people than you want to attend to cover for drop-outs.

Pros

A party selling business is a good way to supplement a regular income and have fun at the same time.

Cons

The business doesn't just revolve around the party itself – you need to be willing to make the first sale but also to follow up on leads and develop relationships, all of which take time.

Useful contact

Information on regulations: www.consumerdirect.gov.uk

Emergency babysitting

What is it?

Being a babysitter is about responsibility as much as childcare. You'll have to ensure babies and children are happy, comfortable and safe and that their needs are taken care of. An emergency babysitter covers the same duties, the difference being you offer your services at short notice and for a temporary period of time, for when a child is sick for example and has to stay at home, when an extra pair of hands is needed, or when parents and carers are let down by other babysitting services.

What's the appeal?

Flexibility and the opportunity to earn money at short notice. It suits those people who can drop things at the last minute and accommodate requests for work at all hours of the day and night, including weekends.

What skills do I need?

You don't need any special training but it will reassure parents and carers if you have done some courses in childcare. Basic first aid skills will also be a plus as is the ability to cope in emergency situations.

What does it cost?

There are virtually no start-up costs – you'll either babysit in your own home and use existing items or you'll be using the home of parents or carers and they should provide everything you need. You might need to cover travel costs.

What can I earn?

You can charge more than typical babysitting rates as you are available at short notice. Rates vary depending on location but can be up to £10 an hour. When setting a rate, consider the number of children you will be looking after – the more there are, the higher your hourly fee should be, and factor in the time of day and the ages of the children.

Any red tape?

There are no specific regulations governing babysitters but if you work for an agency, many will expect you to be Ofsted registered, which is a legal requirement for childminders, and a member of the National Child Minding Association, as well as having had a Criminal Records Bureau check.

Prospects for growth

Advertise your services – there are agencies that specialise in offering emergency babysitting and they can generally negotiate better rates for you. One of the biggest challenges parents and carers face is finding a reliable babysitter. If you establish yourself as one and build up a solid reputation, word of mouth from satisfied parents can be enough to keep you busy.

Tips for success

Every family you babysit for will have different views on childcare so bear in mind what might work with one may not work with another. Decide what locations you are happy to babysit in as it is important that you are comfortable with the arrangement.

Pros

It's a good way to introduce yourself to local parents with the possibility of branching out later into regular childcare.

Cons

With emergency babysitting, work can be irregular. Parents and carers might also have different interpretations of 'short notice' – it's not uncommon to be asked if you can get to someone's house in 10 or 20 minutes, for example, so it's best to concentrate on offering your service to a local area so you can get to places in time.

Useful contact

National Childminding Association: www.ncma.org.uk

Music lessons for small children

What is it?

Introducing small children (those under the age of six) to music lessons will help them to focus on their memory and listening skills. As they are too young to read music at this age, they can learn the physical techniques of playing an instrument, with the piano one of the most common instruments taught to children under the age of six. For babies and children up to three years, you could specialise in songs and movement and use props such as puppets to explore the concept of music.

What's the appeal?

Children are often quick learners so giving music lessons to this age group can be both fun as well as a learning process.

What skills do I need?

You should have the ability to play any instruments you will be teaching as well as having a love for different kinds of music. As young children can often have trouble concentrating, it's essential that you are well organised so you can switch to different tasks quickly if necessary. Patience and good communication skills come in handy too.

What does it cost?

There are minimal start-up costs for this work. You will need a workspace and some chairs as well as any instruments you are planning to teach, although if you are thinking of starting this type of business, it is likely you will already have the instruments.

What can I earn?

Average charges for group lessons are between £12 and £15. For smaller groups using instruments, you can charge £15 per child.

Any red tape?

There are no specific regulations but if you choose to work for a school or other training institution, they will have rules that you will need to adhere to.

Prospects for growth

Music lessons for small children is not a business where you can earn substantial sums, but it will enable you to turn a hobby and love of music into a business.

Tips for success

Word of mouth is essential in this line of work so ask satisfied customers to recommend you. Consider taking up another instrument if you know there is a particular demand for it and you are able to learn it.

Pros

This business can be run from home at hours to suit and it can be quite relaxing teaching movement to music and playing instruments.

Cons

You'll have to maintain a positive outlook and persevere even with the most difficult of students and young children can be physically demanding to teach.

Useful contacts

Advice and resources: www.musicteachers.co.uk
Associated Board of the Royal Schools of Music: www.abrsm.org

Kids' football group

What is it?

The emphasis of many kids' football training sessions is on fun as well as teaching skills such as passing the ball, tackling and scoring. Working as a kids' football trainer involves running training sessions for kids from preschool through to teenage years.

What's the appeal?

You can keep fit on the job and most of the classes are at weekends, or in late afternoons during the week (after school), leaving you free time during the week to explore other opportunities.

What skills do I need?

A love of sport and an ability to inspire and motivate. You'll need to prepare for each session so organisation skills are a must. As the level of players in the team is likely to vary, you'll need to be supportive and enthusiastic, whatever their strengths and weaknesses. Most kids' football trainers have experience in nursery schooling, child health or are qualified Football Association coaches so it helps if you have a background in this area.

What does it cost?

You'll need to source a venue (either indoor or outdoor) where the training can take place. Ask around local schools and sports clubs and see if they are willing to let you use some grounds for training. Children should turn up in their own kit but you will need to provide footballs, which cost from £12.

What can I earn?

This will vary depending on location. Set rates on a monthly, quarterly or yearly subscription fee with a one-off membership fee, so you get money up front. For example you could charge £32 a month for each child for a one hour training session once a week, with half that as a sign-on fee, so it would work out as £96 per quarter plus £16 membership on top. Or you could charge a higher registration fee and a lower, monthly, quarterly or yearly subscription.

Any red tape?

Work involving children requires you to get clearance from the Criminal Records Bureau – known as a CRB check.

Prospects for growth

Building up classes is key to growth as you could run four to five training sessions on Saturdays and Sundays, and split these by age group.

Tips for success

Ask parents at local schools if their kids can join to boost numbers and if they are willing to volunteer to help with training – it can be hard work looking after one team of kids.

Pros

Setting up a kids' football training business can be a very rewarding job as you'll be helping to combat problems like obesity. It's also a good way to meet new people.

Cons

You'll be working antisocial hours – evenings during the week and early mornings at weekends. You might have to deal with team members who are not as talented as others.

Useful contact

Football Association: www.thefa.com

5

Pets

Profile – Dog walker

Who: Eleanore Percival
What she does: Walks dogs
Where: West London
Set-up business: 2005
Initial start-up costs: Minimal – a few hundred pounds

There are many advantages to setting up a dog walking business, such as the exercise and fresh air, but there are also a few hazards you need to be aware of.

'Be prepared to get bitten and watch out for fox poo getting in your hair,' warns Eleanore Percival, aged 37, who set-up dog-walking business, The Fairy Dogmother, in West London three years ago. 'I never imagined when I was a little girl that I would be dealing with poo on a daily basis!'

Eleanore gave up a stressful job in the restaurant management business, where she had worked for 15 years, to launch her dog-walking career, but she says the latter can be just as stressful – something she wished she'd known more about when starting out.

'People think dog walking is a walk in the park but there are so many heart-stopping moments, such as when a dog runs out in front of a car,' she says. 'People rely on you too so it's difficult to take a day off or call in sick.'

Eleanore works seven days a week and says she wishes she could make more time for holidays as the work can be both physically and mentally exhausting – her advice for budding dog walkers is to learn when to say no. You also need to look after yourself – Eleanore once broke her arm and couldn't drive, making it difficult to pick up dogs and take them for walks. Being aware of park regulations is essential too as some will allow dogs to be off their leads while others won't.

It's a business, however, that she clearly loves. One of the aspects that Eleanore enjoys most is the training available – she completed a correspondence course in dog behaviour that set her back about £100 and which has proved invaluable.

'I have unconditional love for the dogs and they make me laugh every day,' she says. 'There is so much variety as all the dogs are different, although some days you want the ground to swallow you up, especially when the dogs run off with someone's football. You have to be careful of other people's attitudes, too, especially those with young children. I've given talks, for example on how to approach dogs, as it's important.'

In terms of set-up costs, it helps to have a car and to install dog barriers, as it means you can take several dogs out at the same time, although car cleaning costs can mount up and, in Eleanore's words, the car 'really honks'. Buying snacks and paying for personal and public liability insurance are a must, particularly as you have a set of people's house keys. The other big expense is clothes, which wear out pretty quickly.

'Looking after a dog is like being responsible for someone's child, so you definitely need insurance for peace of mind,' she says. 'You also need to have a certain amount of diplomacy and tact as some customers have some very firm ideas about how to treat their dogs. Often, the challenges are more with the owners than their dogs.'

Eleanore's business has built up over the last three years through word of mouth from local veterinary services and pet shops. Dogs, she says, are also the biggest ice-breaker so when walking, it's easy to strike up conversations with people and perhaps drum up some more business. In terms of fees, she charges £12 for an hour walk, takes between 14 and 20 dogs out a day and has around 70 on her books. Some occasionally stay overnight, for which she charges £25.

It's not all been plain sailing though. Last year, Eleanore expanded the business by taking on a good friend as a business partner, but sadly it did not work out.

'You have to be careful who you employ in this type of business – know your tolerance threshold,' she advises. 'He forgot to take a dog out so I had to let him go.'

Although Eleanore has found it hard to squeeze in the odd holiday, she has managed to get away. But this has not stopped her from offering the best customer service possible.

'You meet so many other dog walkers when out with the dogs that we are like a small community,' she explains. 'If I then go on holiday, I can always recommend another dog walker so there is continuity with my clients and I can still help them.'

And the biggest perk? Eleanore confides that she gets 'brilliant Christmas presents' and some fantastic tips. She also does the odd trade-off with other small business owners – one of her customers is a hairdresser who cuts her hair in return for her walking his dog.

Boarding care

What is it?

It provides a home away from home for animals, typically dogs and cats, offering them quality care and giving their owners peace of mind. You will be looking after animals, feeding them and exercising them, such as taking dogs for walks, often for a specific period of time while pet owners are on holiday.

What's the appeal?

If you love animals this job combines the opportunity to work with them as well as relaxing with them and enjoying plenty of fresh air and exercise. You look after the animals in your own home so the job can be worked around existing commitments.

What skills do I need?

Experience of working or looking after animals is preferable – not only will this inspire confidence in your customers but it will also reassure you that you can cope with looking after different types of animals at the same time. A reasonable level of fitness is necessary as looking after pets can be strenuous and you'll need to be able to remain calm under pressure and be patient too. Having outside space is a plus.

What does it cost?

You will need to provide a space in your home where animals can relax, drink, eat and sleep, such as providing dog baskets (£15) and bowls (£3) – you can buy these or use any existing items you may have such as pillows and blankets. The more professional your facilities look, the greater your appeal – pet owners will want to check the facilities you provide.

What can I earn?

Rates vary depending on location and type of animal. According to the National Association for Petsitters, home dog boarding can attract a rate of between £12 and £15 per dog per 24-hour period. You should charge slightly more for puppies as they will need more care, attention and exercise. Factor in pick up and drop off rates too if necessary.

Any red tape?

Ensure you take out public liability insurance to protect against any accidents. As an operator of boarding services, you'll need to check out the Animal Boarding Establishments Act, which allows local authorities to impose their own terms and conditions and these can vary from region to region.

Prospects for growth

Pet owners prefer boarding services over kennels and catteries as they tend to provide a more personal service and are more flexible. That being said, check out demand in your local area as competition for these services can be strong.

Tips for success

All animals differ and their needs and behaviours vary too. Arrange a consultation period initially with the owners and their pets, to ensure that their requirements match your services – you need to be comfortable with the arrangement and the animal in order to provide the best service.

Pros

Working with animals can be a very sociable job, particularly if you are taking dogs for regular walks.

Cons

Looking after other people's pets in your own home is a huge responsibility – it's not a job that you can switch off from at any time. Looking after more than one dog at a time can be stressful if they don't get on with each other.

Useful contacts

Animal welfare information: www.defra.gov.uk
National Petsitters Association: www.dogsit.com

Petsitting/visits

What is it?

Looking after and caring for animals in your own home or that of the owners, which includes taking them for walks if appropriate, feeding them and looking after them if they are unwell. You might also choose to offer a day care or home visit service.

What's the appeal?

It's a rewarding job that is fun too, as you will be able to earn money from your love of animals.

What skills do I need?

Reliability, trustworthiness (as you will be working in someone else's home), an ability to get on with animals and a caring nature. You will also need to be physically fit if you are taking dogs for walks. Having a background in caring for animals (either by having had your own or looking after others) is useful too and will boost your profile and appeal to potential customers.

What does it cost?

There are minimal costs attached to this type of work as you will be using the pet owners' facilities and equipment. It's a good idea to buy pet snacks for walks, which cost from £1.00 upwards.

What can I earn?

Rates vary – from £50 to £400 a week depending on the services you offer, according to the National Association of Registered Petsitters, which offers the following guide: dog walking/daily visit (£10 per hour), housesitting (minimum of £30 per 24-hour period).

Any red tape?

Most petsitting services do not require any form of licensing. Ensure you cover yourself with public liability insurance to protect against any accidents.

Prospects for growth

Pet owners are keen to use experienced petsitters over friends and family, as they can provide a more professional service. Leaving animals at home alone for a long period of time is also risky so there is likely to be strong demand, particularly in urban areas where animals will need regular exercise and where people have limited access to outside space.

Tips for success

If owners are going to be away for a while, you could add on other services as well as petsitting to broaden your appeal and increase your earnings, such as watering plants and collecting mail.

Pros

You have the flexibility of running this business from home or visiting other people's houses so there is variety involved, and you can choose the hours and locations to suit your day.

Cons

The work involves major responsibility – not just looking after animals but people's homes too. Some animals can behave unpredictably so you will need to be alert at all times to changes in behaviour and respond accordingly.

Useful contacts

National Association of Registered Petsitters: www.dogsit.com
Pet Care Trust: www.petcare.org.uk

Grooming

What is it?

Grooming pets is a service mainly aimed at dog owners, offering washing, drying, nail clipping, flea rinses, aromatherapy and microchipping. You will also be checking for fleas or ticks and looking out for any areas of soreness on the dog's skin.

What's the appeal?

Pet grooming is an important aspect of pet ownership. You will be giving advice and helping pet owners to care for their animals, strengthening the bond between them so the job appeals to those who enjoy responsibility.

What skills do I need?

You need to be able to groom different dog breeds using a range of cutting and styling techniques so it's worth investing time and money in a dog grooming course if you are completely new to this area. They cover issues such as animal welfare, how to clip and groom and handling tips. A love of animals goes without saying as is the ability to calm and control dogs that may be nervous.

What does it cost?

You could set up a salon at home, by converting a garage for example, rent out salon premises, or choose to do a mobile grooming business run from a converted van. In all of these cases, you'll need equipment such as a bathtub (£50) with a shower, shampoos and conditioners (£3–£40 depending on amount), rubber gloves and medicated supplies such as flea rinses, as well as a grooming table (£40) and animal clippers (from £8). Drying tools vary from hand-held dryers (£31) to free standing ones that cost around £250, to drying cages which will set you back around £35.

What can I earn?

What you charge will depend on the type and condition of the dog's coat and the services – basic grooming costs for one dog are between £30 and £40 which covers bathing, conditioning, drying and styling. If you are collecting and delivering you should charge extra on top.

Any red tape?

Public liability insurance is a must and you should be aware of any animal welfare legislation as you will be responsible for the dog while you are grooming it. As you may be using harmful substances, check out the Control of Substances Hazardous to Health Regulations.

Prospects for growth

Many dog groomers run a mobile business, where the dog is groomed in a mobile parlour. If you choose this route, you can expand your customer base by travelling directly to prospective customers. Contact animal rescue centres, pet shops, boarding kennels and vets as these are all potential customers.

Tips for success

Start off by offering dog grooming services before considering expanding to other pets, such as cats.

Pros

Grooming is a rewarding business as you are helping to care for animals and preventing potential illnesses.

Cons

It can be messy and tiring as you will be spending much of your time bending over and moving around.

Useful contacts

Animal welfare: www.defra.gov.uk
British Dog Groomers' Association: www.petcareorg.uk

Dog walker

What is it?

It's more than putting on a leash, taking a dog for a walk and throwing balls and sticks. You need to like being around dogs, be able to understand their needs and be aware of the environment around you and any potential hazards, such as traffic, small children and other dogs. You'll also have keys to the dog owner's home and be expected to collect and take the dog back.

What's the appeal?

It keeps you fit as you get plenty of exercise and fresh air. It's also a great way to meet other people who are walking dogs so it can be quite sociable.

What skills do I need?

You need to be well organised, remain calm under pressure and enjoy the company of dogs, as well as being fit as although you may only be walking, taking a dog out is physically demanding. A background in first aid is helpful too and a caring attitude is a must – the dog may not belong to you but you will need to treat it and look after it as if it does.

What does it cost?

Minimal costs as the owner should have all the equipment necessary but it's a good idea to invest in dog snacks to take on the walk, they cost from £1.00 upwards, as well as poop scoops (£1.49) or plastic bags.

What can I earn?

Typically, dog walkers walk several dogs at any one time for an hour or hour and a half and you can earn around £10 an hour per dog walked.

Any red tape?

Check with your local authority for any restrictions – some specify the number of dogs you are allowed to walk at the same time. Taking out public liability insurance (from £80 to £150) is essential in case of any injuries and there are a number of other rules and regulations to abide by, such as how to control dogs and picking up faeces.

Prospects for growth

Dog walkers are in high demand in cities and urban areas where many people work long hours and live in flats with no access to outside spaces.

Tips for success

Ask friends in your local area who own dogs if they are willing to let you walk them so you can assess whether it's the right job for you. Gauge local interest by advertising in a local paper or pet shops, asking people to contact you. Check out the competition to see if there is enough demand in your area, otherwise you might need to work further afield.

Pros

If you like animals, this is an enjoyable business where you work and have fun at the same time.

Cons

You might need to take the dogs back to your own home at times, so you'd need to be comfortable with doing this. Looking after other people's pets is a great responsibility so ensure you are happy taking this on.

Useful contacts

Your local authority

Guide to rules and regulations: www.thekennelclub.org.uk

Training classes

? What is it?

All animals are different and their behaviour varies wildly too. Training classes, aimed at dogs, can help to instil house manners, social skills, potty training and obedience, using commands such as sit, run, and stop, ensuring that dogs are well behaved and become domesticated. You can offer private classes on a day-to-day basis or board and train, where the animal lives with you for a specified amount of time and completes the training in your care.

✓ What's the appeal?

If you like teaching and animals you can combine the two by offering training classes. The work can be carried out in your own home so it's ideal if you want to look after pets but not on a full-time basis.

What skills do I need?

Patience – dogs learn differently and respond to different methods so you might need to test and try several times. The ability to motivate is necessary too, as is the confidence to handle dogs of different breeds. Training courses are available, such as how to train puppies.

£ What does it cost?

Training courses range from £35 to £200 and books and videos cost from £10 upwards. In terms of equipment needed, this will vary on the dog's needs and might include treat bags (£7.25) and training leads (£4.99). If your own home/ outside space is unsuitable and you cannot use the client's home, you will need to source a venue and pay for the hire. Many dog trainers use local town halls for example.

What can I earn?

This varies depending on what classes you offer, where you are based and whether they are private or group – charge more for the former. Beginners/improvers lessons are normally run in blocks of six weeks, with an average charge of around £75, while residential dog training courses start from around £500. Private sessions can attract fees of £40 per class.

Any red tape?

There are no specific regulations but ensure you protect yourself with public liability insurance.

Prospects for growth

Competition in this market is fierce so ensure you research local demand – contact local veterinary services and pet shops to advertise your services. You can supplement your income by selling dog training products at the classes.

Tips for success

Find out as much as possible about the dogs' personalities from their owners – for example, do they like toys or do they respond to treats and titbits? This will help you to plan your training accordingly.

Pros

Training a dog to be well behaved can take a weight off the pet owners' minds, so the job can be very satisfying. Behaviour differs enormously from dog to dog so the job offers plenty of variety.

Cons

You might have to offer classes at weekends to fit around pet owners' schedules.

Useful contact

The Association of Pet Behaviour Counsellors: www.apbc.org.uk

Sales of pet accessories

What is it?

Pet accessories is big business with many pet owners prepared to pay quite a bit for the latest fashion items for their animals. Accessories range from leashes and collars for dogs, to rabbit hutches and cages to doggy designer bags (made famous by Hollywood celebrities) to custom-made beds. The easiest way to set up this business is online – you can run this from home and you won't have to pay any expensive overhead costs for premises.

What's the appeal?

As an online business, you can work as few or as many hours as you want and fit the work around any other existing commitments.

What skills do I need?

A flair for spotting the latest trends in pet accessories and fashion is essential as these change rapidly. You'll also need to have good communication and negotiation skills. If you are selling online, visual impressions are important so an eye for displaying product pictures attractively is useful.

What does it cost?

The easiest way to set up this business is online as you won't have to pay overhead costs for premises. Website costs vary depending on factors such as functionality and number of pages, for example, from £500 for a basic one to £2,000 plus for added features. Start off small as you can add other features as and when necessary.

What can I earn?

This depends very much on the products you will be selling, what price you can buy the stock for and what mark-up you can achieve on sale. Consider whether you want to concentrate on luxury, upmarket pet accessories or whether you are aiming for the more budget-conscious customer.

Any red tape?

If you are selling goods online, over the telephone or through mail order, you'll need to comply with the Consumer Protection (Distance Selling) Regulations.

Prospects for growth

According to figures in 2008 from research agency Mintel, the market for pet accessories has grown by between 3% and 4% year-on-year, with beautifying treatments and eco-friendly products boosting growth prospects.

Tips for success

Think of areas you can specialise in, such as organic or eco-friendly accessories as this will help to differentiate you from the competition. Visit trade shows to get an idea of new products and popular items and to build networking opportunities.

Pros

Owners have strong emotional ties to their pets, treating them as one of the family so accessories are in strong demand.

Cons

There is a lot of competition in the pet accessories business – not just from other online ventures but from department stores, pet shops and supermarkets.

Useful contacts

Setting up an online business: www.businesslink.gov.uk
International Trade Association of Pet Equipment Suppliers: www.petquip.com

6

Professional Services

Profile – Designer

Who: Pete McCormack

What he does: Graphic designer

Where: London

Set-up business: 2006

Initial start-up costs: £3,500–£4,000

Pete McCormack, 31, studied French at Leeds University but left after a year and returned home to south-west London. For the next few years, he worked at the British Veterinary Association (BVA), the trade union for vets. Having initially taken a temporary position clearing out their storage rooms, he worked his way up over several years to the position of marketing manager. In June 2006, he decided to take the plunge and start a graphic design business, Pete McCormack Design.

It was not a difficult decision to make. 'I've always been interested in design and foreign languages. Having opted for the wrong direction at university, I decided to pursue my design interests,' says Pete. 'In terms of learning the necessary skills, I didn't study graphic design but I was very fortunate to have had the backing of the BVA, which allowed me to train on the job.'

Pete believes that if you are a creative person with a flair for art and design and have the necessary computer skills, then a job in graphic design is an attractive option. To become efficient and successful at the job though it helps if you have a number of other skills. These include proofreading and copywriting and an interest in marketing. Above all, you must enjoy project managing as the work involves juggling several customers and different types of work, often at the same time.

Pete used his own money to fund the business and cover start-up costs. By far the biggest expense, he says, will be sourcing and buying the equipment needed. He estimates that getting the right computer hardware and software (Pete uses an Apple Mac) is likely to be your biggest capital outlay – budget for approximately £3,500 for a laptop, printer and design software. But that is just for starters.

'You'll also need things like colour swatch books (a collection of swatches that a designer might put together for reference during a project), which will cost around £200, business cards, letterheads and compliment slips, all which could amount to £500,' advises Pete. 'It's a good idea to set up a website as this can help you promote your business. Costs for this vary so ensure you shop around.'

One of Pete's biggest challenges has been adjusting to working alone – although he has a network of people he works with on different projects, starting out without being able to consult others or bounce ideas off other people was tough at times. Working at home has also been quite a steep learning curve. 'It did take some getting used to, with a bit of daytime television getting in the way to start with,' recalls Pete. 'I quickly realised however that if I didn't work hard I wouldn't get paid.'

He now tends to work regular office hours and tries to stick to these to build up a routine and ensure he achieves a good work/life balance. "I actually really enjoy design and the flexibility that being your own boss gives you, as well as not being answerable to anyone," says Pete. There are obviously still distractions, but this would be the same in any office. Working from home also incurs costs such as increased utility bills, although these can be offset against tax, as can the cost of computers and other equipment.

According to Pete, earnings can vary hugely for graphic designers depending on experience and geographical location and he admits that one of the worst aspects of the job is the uncertainty of work. While he may have to juggle a number of projects and clients at times, at others there can be quite a lull, which is why he believes it is important to market the business in the right way. "It is often a case of feast or famine, which can be stressful at times," he adds.

Pete has worked with a range of clients to produce various marketing materials, including brochures, newsletters, annual reports, tickets, invitations and menus. He has also undertaken logo designs, branding and corporate identity work, with clients including The Bauer Publishing Group and The Booksellers Association.

As is the case with many people who start up businesses, the financial and accounting aspects of the work have been challenging. Looking back, he wishes he'd had more knowledge of tax and self-assessment criteria.

'It all seemed like such a mystery to me, having only ever paid tax at source before,' he says. 'But having completed one return, I now know it's not as complicated as I first imagined although I will definitely ask my accountant for help on the next one. It makes sense for me to spend my time earning money doing what I'm good at and then use some of that to pay an expert to do what they're good at.'

The potential rewards of working as a designer continue to spur him on. 'I can easily imagine a stage where I would have to take on staff and expand the business beyond a one-man band to a design agency,' he says. 'It's important to believe in yourself and your skills and persevere through the lean times.'

Tutoring

? What is it?

Additional tuition that provides children and young people (from primary to A-Level) with the attention they can't get in school or college. Tutoring can take place either in the home of the tutor or that of the child, generally after school though sometimes in the daytime for sixth-form students.

✓ What's the appeal?

This is a profession that is ideal for people who need to be at home for certain times of the day – for example people with children. It can be operated from home, although by travelling to your clients you can increase your appeal and income.

🔍 What skills do I need?

You must have a comprehensive knowledge across the complete range of your subject. This means being at least one level in advance of the level you are tutoring. It isn't essential that you are a qualified teacher but having some teaching experience can reassure parents and boost your confidence.

£ What does it cost?

At home, you will need a room with desk and chairs. This shouldn't cost you – as long as you can guarantee not to be disturbed, you can use a dining room table. You will need access to that year's syllabus (around £2) and sample exam papers (50p–£1) and a range of up-to-date, relevant textbooks (£10 upwards).

£££ What can I earn?

Lessons are generally charged by the hour. Fees vary across the country and for different levels but you might charge between £15 and £20 at home plus a few extra pounds for travel.

Any red tape?

There are no specific regulations – although if you register with tutoring agencies to get your business started you will need to adhere to their criteria and they will check your background.

Prospects for growth

This isn't a big money business but it can easily be built up into much more than a part-time one – if you are prepared to work at weekends and longer evenings.

Tips for success

Keep up to date with the curriculum. And as word of mouth is so important, make sure you get on with your pupils and that they get better grades than predicted.

Pros

Good extra source of income that can be made as much or as little as you have time for.

Cons

The work ties up your evenings and is physically tiring because it is intensive.

Useful contacts

Some of the main examination boards:

The Assessment and Qualifications Alliance (AQA): www.aqa.org.uk/

Oxford Cambridge and RSA Examinations (OCR): www.ocr.org.uk/

Edexcel: www.edexcel.org.uk/

Language lessons

What is it?

This may involve teaching a foreign language to students or teaching English to speakers of other languages (teaching English as a foreign language – TEFL). You'll be planning, preparing and delivering lessons to groups or individuals, producing teaching materials, assessing students' progress and keeping records.

What's the appeal?

Language lessons can easily be carried out from home and there are low start-up costs attached. As people will be at varying levels, lessons are varied.

What skills do I need?

There are many routes into this job. You could have an existing degree in a foreign language, and then acquire a postgraduate qualification in teaching, could have studied education at undergraduate level or could be a native speaker of the language. If you want to specialise in TEFL, there are numerous courses you can take and if you are teaching a foreign language, you'll need to have near-native ability in that language. You'll also need plenty of patience, an understanding of grammar and the ability to explain things clearly and concisely to your pupils. It helps to have a lively personality as you'll need to inspire and motivate students.

What does it cost?

TEFL courses cost from £395 to £900 depending on location and whether you choose distance learning or on-site tuition. You might need to invest in language books and discs (costs from £15), as well as a CD player. Other than that, you will need a desk and chairs.

What can I earn?

If you do individual classes, you can earn around £25–£35 an hour, although rates vary depending on location and the level you are teaching.

Any red tape?

There are no specific regulations but if you decide to work for a language school, you will need to abide by their code of conduct. You will need an enhanced Criminal Records Bureau disclosure if you are considering working with children or vulnerable people.

Prospects for growth

This isn't a business that is likely to grow into a big one, but word-of-mouth is critical for building contacts.

Tips for success

Carry out an assessment of pupils' abilities at the first meeting, so you can assess their levels and tailor the lessons and materials accordingly.

Pros

You can work flexible hours and if you are teaching foreign languages, it helps you to keep your skills up to date.

Cons

You'll have to spend time preparing lessons and materials so the work is not just confined to lesson times. Some students may not be very talented at learning languages and it can be difficult dealing with such cases.

Useful contact

International Association of Teachers of English as a Foreign Language: www.iatefl.org

Music lessons

What is it?

If you have a talent for singing or playing a musical instrument, you could pass this onto others through music lessons. You can teach private lessons on a one-to-one basis or carry out lessons with small groups of people, either in your own or your pupils' homes. You can also specialise in reading and interpreting music or help people to prepare for music exams.

What's the appeal?

It provides work that is both challenging and rewarding, offering high levels of job satisfaction as well as responsibility.

What skills do I need?

Many music teachers are professional musicians so you should already have proficiency in instruments or singing. You should also have an academic background, such as a degree in music or a diploma. You'll also need to have a passion for music and the ability to motivate and inspire students, including those who may struggle.

What does it cost?

There are minimal start-up costs as you are likely to already own the instrument you will be teaching. You might have to invest in textbooks, sheet music and songbooks, which cost from £10 upwards.

What can I earn?

According to the Incorporated Society of Musicians (ISM), the UK's professional body for musicians, fees for private lessons can range from £9 to £70, depending on location and the type of lesson offered, and whether it is targeted at adults or children.

Any red tape?

There are no specific regulations, but if you join a member body such as the ISM, you will be required to abide by a code of ethics and a code of practice to ensure the quality of its services to pupils.

Prospects for growth

Experience and contacts can go some way towards boosting your profile so word-of-mouth marketing is important. Consider combining private teaching with part-time or casual work for colleges and other organisations involved with music.

Tips for success

It's a competitive industry so you will need to be both determined and dedicated for the business to take off.

Pros

You can choose the hours you want to work so you can do as little or as much as you want. The business can easily be run from home although you are likely to expand your customer base if you are prepared to travel.

Cons

Training in music is a long-term process so it can take time for your pupils to see results and for you to benefit from repeat work. You'll be teaching people of all abilities and will need to have patience, tact and perseverance to deal with those who are less musically talented but who still want to learn.

Useful contacts

Incorporated Society of Musicians: www.ism.org
Training opportunities: www.abrsm.org

Computer skills lessons

What is it?

Computers and IT are an essential part of modern life, and with new technologies and software being released on a regular basis, it's important to be as up-to-date with these packages and acquire new skills where necessary. Providing lessons in computer skills involves teaching everyone from basic to advanced level, so you might be helping people to create simple documents one day and teaching an advanced software package the next. You might also find yourself helping people to set up computers they have recently purchased.

What's the appeal?

A love of sharing your knowledge and expertise and an interest in computers and IT, together with a desire to keep on learning, as you will need to undertake courses yourself to keep up to date with changes in technology.

What skills do I need?

Patience and an ability to tailor lessons to individual requirements. You'll need an in-depth knowledge of computer skills, be able to explain complex information clearly and concisely and have good interpersonal skills. The ability to motivate and inspire is useful too.

What does it cost?

There are minimal set-up costs attached. If you are offering lessons from home, you'll need a couple of computers, desk and chairs and perhaps some textbooks, which can cost from £10. Software packages will probably be your biggest investment (up to £1,000 depending on what you teaching).

What can I earn?

Rates vary but you can charge between £15 and £20 an hour depending on the levels you are teaching.

Any red tape?

There are no specific regulations, but if you intend to work with children and vulnerable people you'll need clearance from the Criminal Records Bureau.

Prospects for growth

IT training is a fast-growing industry so there is demand but the competition is strong, which is why personal recommendations are a must for this business. Consider tapping into local schools and adult education centres to advertise your services. You could choose to specialise in certain software packages too, to increase your appeal.

Tips for success

Assess the needs of potential students so you can tailor lessons appropriately. For example, some people will want to learn computer skills for work purposes, others will be doing it for personal reasons, such as surfing the internet or sending emails and you may be preparing others for exams.

Pros

You can increase your professional development on the job as you can enhance your skills as you teach.

Cons

You will be working with computers for most of the time, so this could put a strain on your eyes. Some pupils will not pick up skills as quickly as others but you'll need to accept that some are more gifted than others.

Useful contact

Institute of IT Training: www.iitt.org.uk

Secretarial services

What is it?

Providing administrative and clerical support to businesses remotely, via telephone, email and post, including typing documents, updating records, using software packages, invoicing and transcribing tapes. You might also be required to take notes during conference calls and arrange meetings and travel.

What's the appeal?

The role is suited to those who like to work independently and the work can easily be carried out from a spare room at home.

What skills do I need?

If you choose to specialise in a certain field, such as law or medicine, you will need to have a relevant qualification. If you are offering general secretarial services, competent typing skills are a must, alongside the ability to be organised and meet deadlines as you must be able to plan and prioritise your workload. Communication skills, in particular a good telephone manner, proficiency in grammar and spelling and accuracy are vital too.

What does it cost?

Start-up costs are minimal – you'll need a computer, printer and internet connection and additional equipment such as stationery, inks and envelopes.

What can I earn?

This varies depending on the type of work you undertake and location. For general secretarial services, charges are between £15 and £20 an hour. Factor in costs such as postage and add these on top. For work requiring a shorter turnaround you could consider charging more.

Any red tape?

There are no specific regulations but for jobs which require a lot of time, it's wise to draw up a contract specifying what services you will provide, over what time and for what rate.

Prospects for growth

There will always be a demand for secretarial services but competition is strong. If you build up a number of regular clients, you could generate a sizeable amount of work. Tap into local businesses to see if there is any 'overflow' work that you can provide – if you do a good job of this, it will help get you noticed and generate further projects.

Tips for success

Consider any extra skills you can bring to the table to improve your chances of success, such as foreign languages, software packages, a head for figures or experience of a particular sector. If you have a flair for foreign languages, for example, you could consider tapping into an overseas customer base.

Pros

As a secretary, you can work across many different types of industry at the same time, adding variety to the work.

Cons

Competition is stiff as it's a relatively easy business to set up so it will take time and effort to get the business off the ground.

Useful contact

Institute of Qualified Professional Secretaries: www.iqps.org

Personal assistant services

What is it?

Personal or virtual assistants offer one-off or regular administrative services to businesses and individuals on a remote basis, including dealing with emails, answering phones, taking minutes at meetings, dealing with correspondence, booking travel and organising appointments. As a personal assistant, you will provide clients with a more personalised and individual service than that of a secretary, which tends to focus on more general tasks.

What's the appeal?

The work can easily be carried out at home but as you are in constant contact with your clients, it is not as lonely as other home-based jobs can be. It's a job that suits those who have previous experience in administrative support.

What skills do I need?

Virtual assistants are highly experienced people, who have built up a good track record in previous administrative roles. Good communication skills are a must, particularly a confident telephone manner, alongside the ability to be well organised and have an excellent awareness of time and deadlines. You'll also need to be able to multitask, as you will be dealing with various clients at the same time. You'll need to be flexible and accommodating too as you may be asked to do tasks at short notice and within a tight time frame.

What does it cost?

You'll need a computer with internet access, a phone (separate from your land line) and a fax.

What can I earn?

The more specialised your skills are, the more you will be able to charge. Typical rates are between £15 and £25 an hour, depending on the type of service you are providing.

Any red tape?

There are no specific regulations but cover yourself with professional indemnity insurance. If you join an organisation such as the Society of Virtual Assistants, you will need to abide by their code.

Prospects for growth

A virtual assistant frees up time for busy businesses and individuals that they can better spend elsewhere, so you should emphasise this when pitching for business. Consider doing a trial service to get your business up and running by offering services to friends and family and asking them to recommend you.

Tips for success

Ensure you agree in writing precisely what work is to be carried out, the timescales involved and the cost, as the majority of your work is completed without ever meeting the client. Decide up front how you will bill for the work, such as on a weekly, monthly or project basis and what other costs might need to be factored in, such as postage.

Pros

You can work for a range of clients in different sectors so although many of the tasks you perform may be the same, the industries will be different, offering variety.

Cons

You need to be available outside of normal office hours and be able to turn tasks around at short notice, so the job can be stressful at times. Clients will expect you to be available most of the time.

Useful contact

Society of Virtual Assistants: www.societyofvirtualassistants.co.uk

Writing

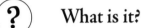

What is it?

Receiving an hourly rate or fixed fee in return for writing. This could include features and articles for magazines and newspapers, marketing materials, books and pamphlets. You'll also research themes and pitch these to potential clients.

What's the appeal?

Work is normally carried out in your home, although you might be expected to work at the client's site on occasion. This job is suited to those who crave flexible working hours as you can work the hours you want, as long as you meet deadlines.

What skills do I need?

Self-discipline is the key to success, as hitting deadlines is one of the most important aspects of writing. Specialist know-how can also help you to stand out from the competition and you need to be a dab hand at scheduling and organisation.

What does it cost?

Most freelancers work from home so the start-up costs are minimal – a bedroom converted to an office, with a desk, computer and internet access, a telephone and an answering machine plus a fax machine. You'll also need business stationery and business cards for advertising yourself to clients. As a rule of thumb, it will cost £1,000–£1,500 to set yourself up.

What can I earn?

This will depend on what you charge, how fast you work, and how many hours you put into the business. For example, a reasonably successful freelance writer would typically charge £200 per thousand words and would expect to research, interview and write up at least one 1,000-word feature per day. So you could earn around £1,000 a week.

Any red tape?

No specific regulations but you will need to adhere to all the usual rules and regulations of self-employment.

Prospects for growth

Most freelance writing work is obtained via word-of-mouth so networking is an important aspect of building contacts and securing work. Look beyond your existing clients and ask them to spread the word.

Tips for success

Successful scheduling can mean turning work away. It's very tempting to just take on everything that's offered to you, but you've only got to miss a deadline or deliver substandard work once and you've got an unhappy client who's going to go elsewhere next time around. It's important that you have separate lines for your phone, fax and internet access so you can be contacted easily at all times and maintain levels of professionalism.

Pros

Variety – you can choose to work for several different clients at the same time, covering different subjects. This also lessens the risk of unemployment.

Cons

Most freelancers face the major worry of getting enough work. You may not be fully employed, week in and week out, especially when starting off. Getting paid on time is another problem.

Useful contacts

Writers' Guild: www.writersguild.org.uk

National Association of Writers in Education: www.nawe.co.uk

Ghostwriter

What is it?

Writing books, articles, stories and reports and allowing someone else to put their name to it, so the work is officially credited to another person. It's a technique commonly used by celebrities, politicians and other people in the public eye when they wish to release an autobiography or their memoirs.

What's the appeal?

You enjoy writing and you don't mind the fact that your name and byline won't appear.

What skills do I need?

A passion for writing and understanding the subject matter are a must but personal qualities are often more important, namely discretion, as you are likely to be privy to intimate details of people's personal lives. You'll need to be highly organised as you'll be expected to take copious notes and recordings and transcribe this into coherent material. You'll need to have the ability to put yourself in your subject's shoes and imagine them as the author of the book.

What does it cost?

Start-up costs are minimal. You'll need a computer and phone, recording equipment and stationery.

What can I earn?

This depends on the type of writing you are undertaking and how it will be used. For example, you could be writing a piece that is not meant for the wider world, in which case negotiate a fixed fee. If the work is for publication, consider a lower fixed fee for a percentage of any potential royalties earned when the book is published.

Any red tape?

You will be expected to sign a confidentiality agreement if you are penning work on behalf of a celebrity or someone in the public eye. Ensure a contract is drawn up with terms and conditions that suit both parties.

Prospects for growth

Contacts are all important in this line of work, particular if you want to operate at the more lucrative end of the market. Consider specialising in certain areas – such as writing business autobiographies or celebrity memoirs – as you can then build up a reputation in these areas.

Tips for success

Successful ghost writing is very dependent on the relationships you build with your clients and establishing a good rapport. Arrange an initial meeting with the client to see if you both get along and have a good working relationship. At the end of the day, the piece needs to come across as having been written by the client.

Pros

The work can easily be carried out from home as most of it can be done over the phone, with a few face to face meetings.

Cons

It can take several months from start of the project to completion so factor these timings in when accepting/looking for work so you can organise your time efficiently. The work is likely to go through several drafts so account for these timings too.

Useful contact

Resources: www.writersservices.com

Copywriter

What is it?

Providing written content to promote products and ideas across a variety of formats, such as adverts, websites, brochures, radio commercials, leaflets and posters. You'll also be checking and revising work where necessary and coming up with ideas following a brief from clients.

What's the appeal?

There's plenty of variety and creativity and you need to be able to adapt your mind to a range of different subject matters and formats.

What skills do I need?

Excellent spelling, punctuation and grammar go without saying and you need to have a good grasp of words and be able to use them to inform people, writing persuasive and eye-catching copy in a range of styles. Good communication skills are vital as you will be liaising with a number of people as part of the copywriting process. Meeting deadlines is essential too.

What does it cost?

You'll need a computer, phone and internet connection, so start-up costs are minimal. Initial face to face meetings with clients are usual, so factor in travel costs.

What can I earn?

This varies greatly, depending on geographical location and what medium you are working on. Copywriters tend to charge around £40 an hour or a fixed day rate, which could be anything from £200 upwards.

Any red tape?

There are no specific regulations but you need to protect yourself with professional indemnity insurance.

Prospects for growth

It's a competitive industry but the growth of the internet means it is one of the biggest markets for copywriters – particularly in areas such as writing copy for search engine optimisation and e-marketing. It might be worth investing in a course specialising in this area so you can broaden your skills and appeal.

Tips for success

Clients will want to see proof of your creativity and writing ability so build up a portfolio with examples of your work, even if you have not yet been published. The relationship you have with a client can make the difference between success and failure so ensure you address any potential conflicts early on. Ensure you meet all deadlines as this can make the difference between being hired for repeat commissions or the client looking elsewhere.

Pros

You can get a real buzz from seeing your idea become reality and knowing that you have helped people to view a product or issue in a different light.

Cons

A piece of work you think is good might not be so well received by the client, so you need to be able to take criticism and start all over again. The pressure of meeting deadlines may involve some late nights and work at weekends.

Useful contacts

Advertising Association: www.adassoc.org.uk
The Communication Advertising and Marketing Education Foundation: www.camfoundation.com

Public relations

? What is it?

Helping to build a company's reputation. You could be writing and editing press releases and other corporate communications material, organising events on behalf of a client, helping to develop and maintain a business' corporate identity and working on media relations building up contacts with the media.

✓ What's the appeal?

The variety of the job – you could be organising events, writing, helping on marketing materials and liaising with journalists.

🔎 What skills do I need?

Excellent people skills are a must, as well as good written skills and the ability to convey complex information precisely and concisely. You need to be able to work well under pressure and meet deadlines as well as having creativity and initiative. Accuracy and attention to detail is a must too, as is multitasking, as you will be juggling several clients at the same time.

£ What does it cost?

Start-up costs are minimal – you'll need a computer, internet access and phone. You'll be travelling to meet clients face to face for initial meetings but much of the work can be carried out over the phone. Investing in marketing and stationery will help to boost your profile.

£££ What can I earn?

According to the National Union of Journalists, rates vary hugely. As a rough guide, it suggests that consultancy work for a day can attract around £320, or a retainer fee of £1,200 per month. Press office work per day can net around £330. You could also charge a fee (around £15) per day to cover operational costs, such as telephone, email and postage.

Any red tape?

Ensure you take out professional indemnity insurance.

Prospects for growth

Word of mouth is an important way of getting referrals in PR – build a rapport with clients, gather testimonials and keep evidence of campaigns, press releases and events you have worked on and the results you have achieved. If you have gained coverage for a client in the press, for example, it's worth keeping a folder of cuttings that you can show to potential clients.

Tips for success

Consider doing some volunteer PR work to assess if it is the right move for you, by contacting friends and family and seeing if they have some work for you. Decide if there are some areas you are particularly good at, such as writing or organising events, as you may want to highlight these to potential clients if relevant.

Pros

This business can be easily run from home but can also involve meetings and sociable events in the evening so offers workplace variety.

Cons

Competition is fierce – PR ranks as one of the top three most popular career choices for graduates in the UK, according to the Chartered Institute of Public Relations.

Useful contacts

CIPR: www.cipr.co.uk
Public Relations Consultants Association: www.prca.org.uk

Editing and proofreading

What is it?

Ensuring that texts that are due for publication in print and on the web are well written and grammatically correct. You could find yourself working across a variety of media, including books, magazines, newspapers, journals and online material. You could be correcting spelling errors, flagging up sections that are not clear, checking facts and figures and making sure the style of the piece is consistent.

What's the appeal?

The work can easily be done from home and is creative – you'll also be able to work for several different clients at the same time so there is variety involved.

What skills do I need?

There are no specific qualifications required but you'll need to have an excellent grasp of the language you are working in, accuracy and attention to detail, the ability to multitask and good concentration. A certain amount of tact and diplomacy can come in useful as you'll need to persuade clients why you believe some changes are necessary. There are a variety of courses to choose from if you are completely new to the sector.

What does it cost?

You'll need a computer, internet connection and phone so there are minimal costs involved. Courses start from £200.

What can I earn?

According to the Society for Editors and Proofreaders, you can expect to earn the following per hour as a minimum: proofreading, simple indexing: £19.25; copy-editing, creative indexing (paper): £20.75; on-screen copy-editing: £22:50; substantial editing and rewriting: £26.00; project management: £28.00.

Any red tape?

There are no specific regulations but ensure you are covered with professional indemnity insurance.

Prospects for growth

It's a competitive industry and according to the Society for Editors and Proofreaders the most successful way to generate work is through contacts and networking. If you join, you can get access to directories offering work. Send your CV out to potential clients and other contacts in the industry.

Tips for success

If you have expertise in a niche sector such as engineering or natural sciences, you may find it easier to get work as these areas rely on good levels of knowledge of subject matter. Foreign language skills might come in useful too. Research and approach smaller publishers as they may be more willing to give you work if you are new to the market.

Pros

If you work for several clients at the same time, you can generate a small income and the flexibility means you can fit it around other commitments.

Cons

You might have to deal with clients who insist on making changes and asking you to do revisions over and beyond what you are contracted to.

Useful contact

Society for Editors and Proofreaders: www.sfep.org.uk

Graphic designer

What is it?

Developing identities, designs and logos for products and services, working in areas such as advertising, book, magazine and newspaper publishing, packaging, marketing and web design. You'll be conveying ideas through visual design techniques, including illustration, computer graphics and photography.

What's the appeal?

Taking ideas from concept to reality can be immensely satisfying and you'll be liaising with a number of people for each project so the job suits those who like working independently but also as part of a team.

What skills do I need?

Creativity, imagination and a flair for creating original work is essential. You'll need to come up with ideas and put these into practice and work to deadlines set by clients. Work is normally based on any past experience rather than academic qualifications. Good communication skills are essential as you'll be meeting with clients to discuss briefs and you'll need to have a good knowledge of software packages such as InDesign, Dreamweaver, Acrobat, Illustrator, Photoshop and Flash. You will need to be confident pitching your ideas to clients.

What does it cost?

Set-up costs can be in the region of £3,000, as you'll need a computer, printer and design software. Factor in marketing costs such as business cards and stationery and this could add another £500 on top.

What can I earn?

Rates vary depending on location and project but you can expect to earn up to £40 an hour.

Any red tape?

Take out professional indemnity insurance. You should ensure contracts are drawn up for all work so you are aware of what your requirements are and the client's brief.

Prospects for growth

Many graphic designers find work through word of mouth, so networking is important. Depending on the sector you choose to specialise in, send samples of your work to prospective clients as they may have 'overflow' work initially that can develop into more regular work.

Tips for success

Create a portfolio of your work to show to potential clients. It will be to your advantage to invest in a website where potential clients can find out more about you and the companies you have worked for, particularly if you wish to specialise in web design.

Pros

The range of industries you can work in – from publishing companies to advertising agencies to the printing and packaging industry. If you choose to specialise in internet opportunities, you could train as a web designer. Software packages are updated regularly so there are many on-the-job training opportunities.

Cons

Clients may not be satisfied with your designs, so you need to be able to take criticism and be accommodating. The work might need to go through more stages than detailed in the contract so be prepared to work long hours to meet deadlines.

Useful contact

Chartered Society of Designers: www.csd.org.uk

Collection agency

What is it?

Setting up a collection agency involves recovering money from overdue accounts from businesses or individuals. You'll be investigating and keeping records of reasons for non-payment, preparing relevant correspondence, highlighting problems and reviewing the cases of those who have promised to pay on a regular basis to ensure they do so. The majority of collection is done by post and telephone but human intervention is sometimes required.

What's the appeal?

It's for those who like to communicate by telephone and written correspondence, and who do not shy away from confrontational situations. You could find yourself visiting debtors to collect payments, known as 'field collection' so you need to be confident doing this.

What skills do I need?

There are no minimum academic qualifications required. Excellent communication skills, a professional telephone manner and the ability to negotiate are essential as you will need to work out repayment terms. You also need to be assertive, as you will be dealing with difficult customers, and able to remain calm under pressure. Good numerical skills go without saying.

What does it cost?

A driving licence, car and phone are necessary if you want to get involved in field debt collection. You'll also need a computer and internet connection to keep accurate records and complete correspondence, as well as a printer.

What can I earn?

You could charge a percentage of debts collected or operate on a fixed fee. The older the debt, the more you should charge as it's likely it will take longer to recover. For field collection, pay is usually by commission and so varies from job to job.

Any red tape?

Before being able to operate as a collection agency for the collection of consumer debts (private individuals) a Consumer Credit Licence from the Office of Fair Trading (OFT) is required. Public liability insurance is required if you have office premises and ideally, to cover you for unforeseen professional mishaps, professional indemnity insurance.

Prospects for growth

With the onset of the credit crunch, people are falling into debt more than ever before, but according to the Credit Services Association the market is tough, with small profit margins and very competitive trading conditions. Economic downturns tend to lead to increased reluctance from companies and individuals alike to pay their debts.

Tips for success

Consider whether your focus will be towards consumer or commercial debts, although working in both areas is possible. It is essential to have a clear contract with clients, which should contain an outline of services provided, fees and cover situations such as the withdrawal of accounts by the client.

Pros

You'll be dealing with different people, such as solicitors, bailiffs and debt counsellors and a range of tasks such as tracing missing debtors, recording payments and negotiating terms so there is variety.

Cons

Recovering unpaid money is a sensitive subject and you'll need to be assertive and have a thick skin, as some people will take an immediate dislike to you. If you do field collection, you'll need to work evenings and weekends as this is when most people are likely to be at home.

Useful contacts

Credit Services Association: www.csa-uk.com
Institute of Credit Management: www.icm.org.uk

Driving agency

? What is it?

Becoming a driving instructor is not all it seems. You can't simply get into a car and drive off into the sunset. There is a lot that must happen behind the scenes before you can start taking pupils out on the road and teaching them all they need to know. As a driving instructor, you can set-up on your own business or use a franchise, but in both cases, you will be assessing a learner driver's knowledge and planning lessons based on this.

✓ What's the appeal?

It's suited to those who are practically minded, who are willing to take exams and who can remain calm under pressure.

🔍 What skills do I need?

You have to pass a three-stage exam to become an ADI (approved driving instructor) in order to enter the Official Register of Driving Instructor Training (ORDIT) that the Driving Standards Agency (DSA) holds. Communication skills are all important too, including the ability to empathise and get on with your pupils and create a lasting relationship. A healthy sense of humour and patience are also vital as each pupil has a different character and personality so there will be a new challenge on a daily basis.

£ What does it cost?

If you have your own car, costs are fairly minimal. If not, you will either have to invest in one with dual controls, which could set you back, or be supplied with one if you choose to go to the franchise route. The AA, for example will supply you with a car as well as insurance, road tax and repairs with the only cost being petrol. As well as the latter, the major expense will be training, which can cost between £800 and £2,500.

What can I earn?

Base your income on the cost of the lesson (from £15 to £30 depending on location) and the hours worked. If you represent a franchise, bear in mind how much they charge as part of the fee.

Any red tape?

You must not have been disqualified from driving at any time in the four years prior to entering the Register and you need to have held a full UK or European Union or European Economic Area driving licence for four years.

Prospects for growth

If you start out on your own, it might take time to establish your reputation so expect things to be a bit slower at the beginning.

Tips for success

You can choose to start out on your own. Alternatively you could train with and sign up to a pre-established franchise that already has a list of pupils, contacts and trainers. In both cases you are self-employed but with varying degrees of individuality and support.

Pros

Everyone who has passed their test remembers their driving instructor so the job offers high rates of personal satisfaction.

Cons

Some periods of the year will be busier than others and bad weather can also have an adverse effect on levels of business. You will need to be confident taking risks and not panic in stressful situations.

Useful contact

Driving Standards Agency: www.dsa.gov.uk

Training consultant

What is it?

This is a very diverse industry that can be started in just about any way you want. It can cover anything and everything that can be learnt on a course. There are basically three ways to train people – on site (at clients' premises) or bespoke (specially tailored) and public (less tailored and available to anyone) courses or distance learning (offering courses via the internet, for example).

What's the appeal?

If you are coming straight out of a job where you have worked in one industry for a long time, it may be tempting to become the training maestro for that sector. It helps if you really believe in the benefit of training and empowering others through knowledge.

What skills do I need?

A way with people, a skill and knowledge you would like to share and the ability to explain things clearly and concisely. You also need to be able to motivate and encourage those you train.

What does it cost?

You can get started with a minimum of fuss and with relatively little outlay – your biggest expense is likely to be your car. You should also invest in a PC and printer. Other costs will be your own time and any marketing materials. You could choose to invest in a website (from £500) to promote courses.

What can I earn?

Course costs will vary from £250 per day for basic computing skills but could easily eclipse £1,000 for more customised in-house management training. As a one-man/woman band, you can earn a comfortable wage but you will always be limited by your own time and costs. So expect earnings of £20,000 upwards rather than millions.

Any red tape?

Ensure you are covered with professional indemnity insurance.

Prospects for growth

The more lucrative, and faster-growing end of the market is technical training. This is being driven by advances in technology – particularly the internet. There is a critical shortage of web design and other programming skills.

Tips for success

It is because the industry encompasses a wide range of activities that trainers tend to specialise. Your business is likely to be based on a few key clients coming back for repeat business and them referring you to others. Referrals won't happen unless you really have a passion for what you are doing and offer good customer service.

Pros

Training is an industry that can dip into a large pool of freelance staff so you might choose to expand through associates.

Cons

You will need to constantly update your skills base to ensure you keep up to date with training trends, particularly if you are in a fast-moving environment such as IT.

Useful contact

Training: www.cipd.co.uk

Bookkeeper

What is it?

It involves recording financial information and accounting for money that comes in an out of businesses, so they can track whether they are making or losing money. Tasks are varied – you could be recording day-to-day business transactions such as payments for services or goods, making out invoices, calculating wages, completing VAT returns and checking payroll.

What's the appeal?

Good for those with a head for figures and an enjoyment of number-crunching. Bookkeeping can easily be run from home and suits those who are methodical and organised.

What skills do I need?

Confidence in your maths skills and competence using computers and software packages. Many clients will look for a specific bookkeeping qualification so it makes sense to invest in one. There are plenty of courses available or you can buy textbooks and study from home. Successful bookkeeping relies on developing long-term relationships so you need to have good spoken and written communications skills, together with a high level of accuracy, attention to detail and the ability to meet deadlines. Trust and honesty is important too.

What does it cost?

There are minimal set-up costs – all you need is a computer and internet connection. Your clients will provide all the necessary paperwork (such as invoices and receipts) for you to review. A beginner's bookkeeping course is around £175.

What can I earn?

This depends on location and your clients' needs. According to the Institute of Certified Bookkeepers, you could earn between £10 and £18 an hour but some bookkeepers can charge up to £25 an hour.

Any red tape?

You need to take out professional indemnity insurance (cost depends on level of cover) which protects you against issues such as negligence and loss of documents. You will also need to be aware of certain rules such as Money Laundering Regulations to ensure compliance when working.

Prospects for growth

The law requires every business to provide accounting functions so bookkeepers are always in demand. Referrals are valuable in this line of work so gather as many testimonials as you can.

Tips for success

Research the market for bookkeeping in your local area. Contact accountants in your area to see if they have any need for your services and what rates they are willing to pay. If you have any particular skills, such as accounting software, this will improve your prospects.

Pros

If you build up enough clients, bookkeeping can be a lucrative business to run from home.

Cons

The work can be repetitive and a strain on the eyes as you will be working with a computer for many hours and sifting through paperwork.

Useful contacts

Institute of Certified Bookkeepers: www.book-keepers.org
Financial Services Skills Council: www.fssc.org.uk

Financial adviser

? What is it?

Helping people to choose the most suitable financial products and services for their lifestyle, such as mortgages, investments, pensions and savings. You will build up a picture of people's current financial situation and could work in one of three ways: tied – working on behalf of one company to sell only that company's products; multi-tied – linked to a number of product providers and only offering advice on their products; or as an independent financial adviser (IFA) – choosing products from the whole market.

✓ What's the appeal?

It's a job that commands a tremendous amount of responsibility – not only are you dealing with people's money, but you are also regulated by the Financial Services Authority (FSA).

🔍 What skills do I need?

The ability to build and sustain a strong relationship with the customer, together with a background in sales or finance. You should also have a flair for explaining complex information in a clear and simple manner and an interest in financial products. You'll be required to pass an exam, the Certificate in Financial Planning, the benchmark qualification for financial advisers.

£ What does it cost?

Different modules make up the Certificate in Financial Planning and there are varying costs involved for course materials and exam fees (which range from £54 to £90). Aside from this, you will need a computer and phone to keep records of clients and cover your travel costs.

£££ What can I earn?

You can be paid either by fees (based on an hourly rate) or commission (from the product provider) or a combination of the two. The amount will depend on your clients' wealth, their confidence in you, and your experience.

Any red tape?

The Financial Services Authority regulates the provision of financial advice so you will need to abide by its rules and regulations. Ensure you cover yourself with professional indemnity insurance.

Prospects for growth

People are becoming more and more conscious of the need to control their finances, so specialist financial advice is being sought more frequently. Being an IFA gives you the most flexibility as you are working on behalf of the client. Try and market your services to other professional service providers, such as solicitors and accountants, as they may be able to provide you with some useful leads.

Tips for success

Network with other IFAs to get an idea of the work and to build up contacts. It's a good idea to join trade bodies to keep up to date with developments in the industry.

Pros

As an independent financial adviser, you are free to give the advice you choose, so you can grow the business at your pace and earn as much or as little as you wish.

Cons

People can be cynical about financial advisers so you might need to work hard to overcome negative perceptions.

Useful contact

The Personal Finance Society: www.thepfs.org

Mortgage broker

What is it?

Helping people to find and apply for a suitable mortgage. You will be acting as an intermediary between prospective buyers and lenders, handling sensitive information such as people's finances and advising on the home-buying process, explaining the different types of mortgage available and dealing with mortgage lenders.

What's the appeal?

Your aim is to find the best mortgage deal possible so there is a high element of gratitude from clients and the feeling that you have helped them through what can be a difficult and stressful decision.

What skills do I need?

You don't necessarily need a financial background as you can train from scratch. You'll need an industry-based qualification such as the Chartered Insurance Institute Certificate in Mortgage Advice. Good communication skills, customer service and sales experience and being a 'people' person are more important. The ability to multitask and keep accurate records is important as you will be dealing with more than one client at a time.

What does it cost?

Course fees start from £400. You will need a computer, phone and will have to cover travel costs – most of your work can be carried out from home but for initial meetings, you will need to do these face to face so will have to travel to people's homes or offices.

What can I earn?

You will receive a fee or commission based on finding your customer the best mortgage deal possible, so this will vary depending on the type of transaction.

Any red tape?

As a mortgage broker, you have to follow strict guidelines set down by the regulator, the Financial Services Authority (FSA). Cover yourself with professional indemnity insurance.

Prospects for growth

The current economic climate means it is a challenging time to be a mortgage broker – there are less deals available than in previous years so it can take time to build your reputation. Mortgage scams have been on the rise in recent years too so people may approach you with some cynicism. Establishing a reputation and seeking word-of-mouth recommendations will help overcome this.

Tips for success

The mortgage industry changes rapidly so ensure you keep up to date with new products, financial regulations and economic trends. Training courses are available which can help you to improve your professional development at regular intervals.

Pros

This job can be run easily from home, but as you will be carrying out initial meetings with potential customers face to face, you have the option of combining the two to offer workplace variety.

Cons

You will need to be available at unsocial hours, such as early evenings or weekends, to fit in with customers' requirements.

Useful contacts

Financial Services Authority: www.fsa.gov.uk
Financial Services Skills Council: www.fssc.org.uk
Chartered Insurance Institute: www.cii.co.uk

Market researcher

What is it?

Market research is the process by which new products are developed and involves gauging people's opinions to brands and products, by asking them questions on the street, in focus groups or by carrying out surveys online. You will also be collecting and analysing information.

What's the appeal?

Research methodologies may be not be a fast-moving industry, but no two research projects are the same. As you will be working across different sectors and products, the questions that the research will be looking to answer will vary enormously, offering you variety.

What skills do I need?

Market research involves talking to consumers and businesses so you'll need excellent communication skills. An inquisitive mind and the ability to put people at ease and elicit opinions from them are essential. You'll also need to be objective and be able to take notes and speak in a clear voice. Your appeal will be stronger if you have a solid background in marketing services or research.

What does it cost?

You'll need a computer with internet connection and a phone, so start-up costs are minimal. If you plan on hosting focus groups in your home, you need a space that can seat up to ten people comfortably and recording equipment (a digital recorder costs from around £30).

What can I earn?

This depends on what work you are carrying out and the level of your experience – highly qualified market researchers can charge up to £350 a day for their services. You can earn extra money by hosting focus groups in your home.

Any red tape?

There are no specific regulations but protect yourself with professional indemnity insurance. Be aware of the regulations regarding data protection as you will be asking people a lot of personal questions to see if they are suitable for individual projects.

Prospects for growth

Many market research agencies turn to freelance market research consultants during busy periods or when a certain level of industry knowledge or experience is required.

Tips for success

If you are completely new to the sector, you could contact an agency and start off as a field interviewer (involving street and house-to-house interviewing), which would give you some training. You could also be trained to host group discussions (focus groups) in your home as well as doing telephone interviews, before branching out on your own as a freelance. The Market Research Society has a list of names and numbers.

Pros

Although you will be working on your own, and mostly from home, the job does not seem as lonely as other home businesses, as you are spending much of your time on the phone or interacting with people if you run focus groups.

Cons

You need to build up a regular client base so that the work does not become too irregular but it can take a few months for this to happen.

Useful contacts

The Market Research Society: www.mrs.org.uk
Association for Qualitative Research: www.aqrp.co.uk

Management consultant

What is it?

You will be providing advice and expertise to businesses to address a range of issues, such as helping them to improve their performance, boost levels of staff morale and integrate new divisions. Businesses employ management consultants because they bring a particular set of skills to the company.

What's the appeal?

The opportunity to share your experience and expertise and see your ideas being put into practice. You must be prepared to travel as the majority of work will be carried out at clients' offices.

What skills do I need?

There are no specific qualifications but most management consultants are qualified to degree level and tend to specialise in industries they have worked in before. You'll need to be able to work in a team, have good written and oral skills, be able to solve problems and cope with pressure.

What does it cost?

You'll need to fund your travel to clients' offices, but other than this, a computer and phone are the basic requirements. You'll need to invest in marketing too, such as stationery and business cards.

What can I earn?

Rates vary depending on the project and sector but can range from £250 to £1,500 a day. Ensure you factor in costs such as travel and administration. Some firms may want part of the fees to be based on the results achieved so be prepared to negotiate.

Any red tape?

Professional indemnity insurance is a must – if you join an organisation such as the Institute of Business Consulting, you may be eligible for a discounted rate.

Prospects for growth

Consultants tend to find much of their work through word-of-mouth recommendations so it's vital to build up a solid reputation. You should have an initial consultation with clients before committing to a project to ensure that you understand what is expected of you.

Tips for success

Management consultants can work across a range of sectors, such as strategy, finance, marketing and human resources. Consider which areas best suit your expertise rather than attempting to address a range of issues – the more specialised you are, the more valuable you will be to your clients. Always listen to your clients' views before expressing your own opinions.

Pros

As a management consultant, you'll undertake a variety of projects, with constant challenges and opportunities for personal development.

Cons

Projects can vary in length depending on the type of consultancy you are offering and the needs of the client, so it can be difficult to gauge demand. Relationships might break down over the course of a project so it's important to be aware of any problems and address them sooner rather than later.

Useful contacts

Institute of Business Consulting: www.ibconsulting.org.uk
Management Consultancies Association: www.mca.org.uk

Recruitment consultant

What is it?

Recruitment consultants operate across all sectors of business. They are used by a wide range of businesses – from small businesses looking for temporary cover for their receptionist to big corporations with an annual intake of 1,000 people or more which can't physically deliver that many new employees on their own.

What's the appeal?

The majority of people who become recruitment consultants either already have a background in recruitment, as well as the associated clients, contacts and knowledge of the business; or they have had a career in a certain industry, and think they have the contacts to recruit into that profession.

What skills do I need?

Good sales skills and a confident telephone manner are essential – many people who become recruitment consultants have built up skills in marketing, sales and customer service. If you want to specialise in a certain sector, such as IT or nursing, ensure you have a comprehensive knowledge of the area.

What does it cost?

You can do it fairly cheaply – all you need is a computer and internet connection. As you expand, you'll need access to a CV database (£50–£5,000) and a website to post jobs on, which can cost from £500 to thousands, depending on the functionalities you need and what you are prepared to spend.

What can I earn?

Most recruitment consultants price their services based on whether the employee they are placing is permanent or temporary. For a permanent placement, most recruitment businesses take a percentage of the worker's salary. On a temporary basis, it's more complicated: you will need to factor in the cost of the worker, holiday pay, national insurance, as well as the margin you are looking to take, which will depend on the level you're recruiting on. Some consultants also charge a flat fee.

Any red tape?

There are various rules and regulations to be aware of, such as The Employment Agencies Act, which covers issues such as employing candidates under 18 and recruiting from abroad.

Prospects for growth

There are various ways to diversify your income – some people branch out into HR consultancy, going into companies and managing the entire HR process.

Tips for success

Excel in service – most clients will value good service above everything else, so even if you don't manage to fill the vacancy, both candidates and recruiters will remember you for your level of service. Join a recognised association as this will instil confidence in clients.

Pros

Some of the work will be office/home-based, but you can expect to travel when visiting clients.

Cons

Long hours are inevitable, so commitment to the job is essential.

Useful contact

Industry body: The Recruitment and Employment Confederation: www.rec.uk.com

Marketing consultant

What is it?

Marketing is about promoting a product, service or message to as many people as possible, using a range of techniques such as direct mail, email, word of mouth, promotions and advertising. As a consultant, you'll be analysing marketing data and market research, identifying the best target markets and how to reach them and helping to devise advertising campaigns.

What's the appeal?

It's a creative role and it can be immensely satisfying seeing some of your ideas go from concept to a reality viewed by consumers. You can carry out some of the work from home but you'll need to travel to clients to attend initial briefings and present your ideas.

What skills do I need?

You know what makes consumers tick. To attract clients you will need to have previous and solid experience in marketing or advertising, coupled with sound communication and speaking skills. The confidence to sell your ideas to your clients is also essential, together with attention to detail and a flair for presenting.

What does it cost?

You'll need a means of transport, computer, internet connection and phone. Investing in business cards and stationery will help to boost your profile.

What can I earn?

This depends on location, type of project you are working on and what skills are required – marketing consultants can charge up to £500 for a day's work.

Any red tape?

There are no specific regulations, but ensure you protect yourself with professional indemnity insurance.

Prospects for growth

Marketing is an ongoing necessity – there are always new customers to reach and new products to promote and marketing consultants are needed in almost every industry, so job opportunities are numerous. Internet marketing in particular is flourishing, so you could consider specialising in this area.

Tips for success

You'll need to specialise in certain types of product or markets – such as fast-moving consumer goods, IT, or financial services – and target either the business or consumer market and build a reputation on this. Be clear about what your clients' budgets are from the start so you can plan accordingly. Keep up to date with industry trends, particularly digital marketing as this develops at a rapid pace. Build up a portfolio of your work to show to potential clients.

Pros

You can bring another perspective to a business' marketing plans and question accepted practices, helping them to see things in a new light and make a success of products and services.

Cons

Meeting deadlines is all part of the job so it can be stressful and involve working many hours at certain times of the year when project deadlines are looming.

Useful contact

Chartered Institute of Marketing: www.cim.co.uk

Travel agent

? What is it?

Setting up as a travel agent shouldn't be confused with being a tour operator. The difference is that the former sells the holidays while the latter organises them.

✓ What's the appeal?

You will be actively dealing with people all day either on the phone or in person, which is demanding even if you are naturally interested in people. But if you don't have the stamina or the inclination for this kind of work, becoming a travel agent may not be for you.

What skills do I need?

There are no specific qualifications but you'll need to be highly organised and have a thorough knowledge of the locations you are selling trips to. The role of a travel agent is more about selling advice to your clients than holidays. Your customers want to be reassured they will be able to hire a car, go walking or get vegetarian food, so being able to provide this personal touch will be essential.

£ What does it cost?

It's quite possible to start out as a travel agent from home with a desk, a PC and a telephone line. You can start to build up a client base from friends and family so it isn't technically difficult to get started.

£££ What can I earn?

The travel industry is commission-based so every time you sell a holiday for a tour operator they give you a percentage of the fee. This is where getting your name known will be important, though, as international tour operators aren't going to offer an unknown business favourable rates. Commissions vary a lot.

Any red tape?

By law, you need to provide a bond to reimburse clients if your company should fail financially; this is arranged with a bank or insurance company. Also, you have to have Air Travel Organisers' Licensing (ATOL), which allows you to sell airline tickets. Without it you would be confined to providing accommodation and ground transport only.

Prospects for growth

Joining a trade association will boost your profile in the eyes of your customers, the most widely recognised ones are the Association of British Travel Agents (ABTA) and the Travel Trust Association (TTA). You'll need to abide by codes of conduct if you join.

Tips for success

You won't be able to compete with the big brands on price so it is all about what you can offer over and above that. This is where customer service is important.

Pros

The opportunity to have free or discount holidays as you travel to places combining work and leisure.

Cons

Working as a home-based travel agent is extremely competitive as the internet has enabled people to book holidays themselves, cutting out the services of a travel agent. The industry is also going through tough times at the moment, making the job more challenging.

Useful contacts

Accredited Travel Professional: www.a-t-p.org.uk
Association of British Travel Agents: www.abta.com

Notary

What is it?

A qualified lawyer, and one whose duties are mainly concerned with the verification of documents and information for use in foreign countries. You will be preparing, authenticating and certifying deeds and other documents, for example for purchasing foreign property or certifying documents for people wishing to get married abroad. You will be working for either businesses or individuals.

What's the appeal?

It's a job that commands a good deal of responsibility and trust and is for those with an interest in and understanding of legal matters.

What skills do I need?

You need to have a law degree or be qualified as a solicitor or barrister (although the latter is not an absolute requirement), and then complete the Postgraduate Diploma in Notarial Practices. Good attention to detail, the ability to process complex information, and being able to establish a rapport with people are necessary skills.

What does it cost?

You'll need a personalised seal and pen to witness and sign documents. The diploma (a two-year distance learning course) will set you back around £5,000.

What can I earn?

This depends on the nature of the service as there are no set fees. For less complex matters, average fees for notarial services are around £65. For matters that are more complex and which will require more time, consider charging by the hour, where fees can go up to £200. If documents are needed in an emergency or need to be completed outside of normal office hours, consider charging more.

Any red tape?

Notary work is regulated by the Faculty Office of the Archbishop of Canterbury and there are a number of regulations you need to be aware of, such as renewing your practicing certificate each year. You will also need to be fully insured.

Prospects for growth

In the last few years the need for notarial services has risen as more and more people are investing in foreign properties, there are increased levels of international trade, and people are becoming more aware of personal identity and security issues.

Tips for success

The internet is an ideal place to locate a notary, so you could consider investing in a website to publicise your services.

Pros

A notary's work is global, so you are not restricted to working or practicing in a specific area. As it requires a spread of expertise, the work can be varied.

Cons

As a notary, you need to ensure that your clients bring certain documents with them, such as evidence of their identities and proof of address. You'll also need to verify that clients understand the full implications of all documents, so the work can involve considerable administration and you might need to do some chasing if clients fail to provide the right documents.

Useful contacts

www.facultyoffice.org.uk
www.thenotariesociety.org.uk

7

Creative

Profile – Cake making
Who: Emma Salter
What she does: Cakes, muffins and breakfasts
Where: London
Set-up business: 2002
Initial start-up costs: £1,000

Emma Salter set up her business in 2002, providing home-made organic croissants and muffins for delivery to residents in her local area, as well as party food and cakes for local delicatessens. She was 40 when she launched the business from home, having worked in the film industry for 16 years and been unemployed for a year.

She was put in touch with a start-up support agency, InBiz, and the Portobello Business Centre, her local business advisory service. Cake making wasn't her first choice, however. Emma had originally drawn up a business plan for jewellery making, specialising in tiaras for weddings.

'I figured this would be a recession-proof business, as no matter how hard up people are, they will still spend money on a wedding,' she says. 'But I was advised against doing this and had to think of something else.'

The idea for the business came from Emma's own experience of the film industry, where the norm was working long hours and most weekends.

'I thought it would be appealing, especially for single people who work long hours, to have a home-made breakfast prepared and delivered to them at the weekend when they are exhausted after work,' she says. 'It's a business hard-working professionals would be attracted to.'

Following a successful presentation to the Portobello Business Centre, she received a grant of £1,000 to kick-start the business. This was invested in equipment such as a food mixer and an orange juice squeezer, packaging and producing and printing leaflets for marketing purposes. The A5 leaflets gave information on breakfast menus and doubled as a sign of interest, which people could hang on their doors or put on their window sills. This sign would then alert Emma to potential deliveries as she cycled around a designated number of streets. On her first day of business, the leaflets attracted a 6% response rate.

'I enjoy baking and started making organic croissants, muffins, frittatas and orange juice, to deliver by bicycle from 8am to noon at weekends to residents in my local area,' says Emma. 'I also developed a small sideline making party food and then branched out further into making muffins, cakes and biscuits for local delis.'

'The service was more popular with mothers who had young babies and children and whose husbands worked all hours, who had to get up early but had little time to prepare breakfast,' she says. 'Elderly people too were interested as they also get up early.'

Logistics proved to be a problem as on some days, Emma found it a struggle to keep up with demand. The summer months have also proved a slow time for business, as people are away on holiday or tend to get up later. 'I was getting to people's places late and finding out that they had already gone out and got breakfast, so I missed out on sales,' she said. 'I wish I'd started off by targeting a bigger area or got a partner on board so I could have covered more ground.'

In terms of skills, Emma believes that basic accounting, cooking ability and lots of energy for cycling are essential for her business. She also designed flyers to promote the business, putting them through people's front doors, so some design skills came in useful too. Tapping into local contacts and brokering beneficial deals was invaluable in the early days of the business.

'My local vicar let me use the church kitchen for free in exchange for any left-overs being donated to the congregation,' explains Emma. 'This was particularly useful as it was licensed for producing food, so I didn't have to worry about finding premises or any health and safety issues.'

The downside has been the fact that making money from the business has been a challenge – Emma sometimes makes as little as £2 an hour after all the costs, such as ingredients and printing, have been deducted. Providing cakes for local delis and restaurants has been more lucrative, as Emma receives a set amount of funds regardless of whether the shop sells all the cakes. Her work has also led to a couple of catering contracts.

It's not a business, however, for those who shy away from early starts – Emma is up and ready at 3am to start baking – not to mention the prospect of having to cycle in bad weather. Getting to know local people in the area, hearing their feedback and providing a service that they welcome however, has made it worthwhile.

Antiques

What is it?
It's not just a question of having a good eye for relics. Being in the antiques trade involves a lot of detective work. You also need an incredible amount of specialist knowledge and must be prepared for a lot of waiting around.

What's the appeal?
People generally go into antiques because they love them, rather than to make millions.

What skills do I need?
To get your knowledge you need to start doing some detective work. Read, read, read and carry on reading. Go to auctions, antique fairs and other dealerships and look at what's on sale. Lurk at the back and observe how the experts do it.

What does it cost?
Typical running costs for an antiques dealer will be antique fairs stand costs, insurance, car upkeep costs, petrol costs plus phone and mailing costs. Stands at antique fairs can vary considerably. Table top church hall type fairs cost around £60 a day, a bigger county type fair can be anywhere between £400 and £5,000 per stand, whereas the big national events can be as much as £20,000.

What can I earn?
When it comes to pricing you have to consider numerous factors, such as the economic climate, the location, the condition of the antiques, and their scarcity. Don't rely solely on the many price guidebooks on the market. Most price guides are, at best, a starting point and it takes experience and knowledge to price properly.

Any red tape?
There are no special licences required to trade as an antiques dealer, but some councils require that antique shops register with them before setting up, so check

with your local authority. You'll also need to think about insurance as it's vital you protect your goods against fire, theft or any other kind of damage.

Prospects for growth

Specialising in antiques is not a short-term profit-making venture. Antiques can sometimes sell well if they're at a good price, or they can sit for months, if not years, with few interested customers.

Tips for success

If you can find a niche like coins, early 20th-century furniture, art deco, art nouveau or Second World War memorabilia, then you already have an edge. But remember what you make up for in lack of competition you lose in possible buyers as the smaller the niche the smaller the available clientele. Once you've decided on the type of antique you're going to sell, you have to become an expert and get your stock together.

Pros

Dealing in antiques involves travelling to fairs so you can combine business with a holiday.

Cons

Getting enough stock is a very long and involved business, so for some people, antiques are only a sideline to their usual occupation.

Useful contacts

The Association of Art and Antique Dealers: www.lapada.org
British Antique Dealers' Association: www.bada.org

Sewing repairs

What is it?

Sewing repairs covers a variety of jobs: you could specialise in alterations and clothes repair, adjusting curtains, drapes and quilts, or concentrate on a specific market, such as bridal wear.

What's the appeal?

Sewing appeals to those who are good with their hands, who are methodical and have an eye for design. It's an enjoyable job for those who like fixing items that can be quite fiddly. It's a business that can easily be run from a room in your home and can be carried out at any time of the day so you can fit sewing around other work commitments.

What skills do I need?

A natural flair for sewing as well as patience and attention to detail as sewing work requires detail and precision. You should also have a good idea of the right material to use for specific products as customers will be looking to you for advice.

What does it cost?

Your biggest outlay will be a sewing machine, which can cost anywhere from £100 to £2,500 depending on its features. Some computerised machines, for example, can help you create embroidery designs which will be useful for making alterations to bridal wear. You'll also need basic equipment such as measuring tapes, cutting scissors, pattern makers, needles and thread.

What can I earn?

Prices vary depending on the type of sewing repairs you choose to specialise in and whether you will be expected to provide materials, for which you would charge more. If the materials are provided, you should charge by the hour. For general alterations, for example, rates start from £8 an hour. For more specialised work such as wedding dress alterations, you can charge depending on what is needed. Rates typically start from £50.

Any red tape?

There are no specific regulations but ensure you draw up a contract for costly jobs, or those where you will be dealing with expensive materials, such as wedding dresses.

Prospects for growth

Consider expanding your customer base by offering your services to dry cleaners in your area.

Tips for success

You may find yourself skilled at several types of sewing repairs but it's a good idea to specialise in one or two areas first, to avoid spreading your services too thinly. Word-of-mouth marketing is a good way to advertise your business so satisfied customers should be your top priority.

Pros

If you have a talent for sewing more intricate items, such as altering bridal outfits, there is a big demand, which will help generate a steady income.

Cons

Sewing work is very methodical so it can become repetitive and bear in mind you will be sitting down most of the time and putting strain on your eyes.

Useful contact

Directory of sewing services: www.craft-fair.co.uk

Crafts

What is it?

An example of this is a blown glass design business which involves designing and making individual glass awards, vases, bowls, paperweights and commissioned sculpture. Other types of craft businesses include candle and soap making, card making, textiles, knitting and needlecraft.

What's the appeal?

Working with people to design something that they want and then physically constructing it. There are definite enjoyable aspects to the job.

What skills do I need?

Design training either from a university or college to give you the formal practical skills. Susan Nixon of Susan Nixon Design spent over two years on a glass blowing scholarship, demonstrating in a museum. Learning in someone else's business can be invaluable practical experience, as well as giving you the opportunity to ask questions and perfect your skills. Candle making courses can be done for as little as £15 and many are run in the evening over two hours.

What does it cost?

Varies but to go into a glass blowing business it is possible to rent a studio one day a week (around £130) to blow the glass and give yourself enough work for the rest of the week. Susan established a workshop for under £4,000 including £500 for a compressor and £500 for a sandblaster. Prices for a good candle making kit, which includes some wick, scent, a mould and instructions costs from around £12 so you can buy a basic kit and try the craft before investing in more sophisticated products. You'll also need a thermometer.

What can I earn?

If your glass blowing pieces are commissioned, for example, they will be sold directly. Otherwise trade shows are the main market. Studio glassware starts at around £20 rising to thousands. For exclusive pieces, expect £150 upwards, and around £100 for retail vases.

Any red tape?

If the craft involves a workshop you need to observe certain health and safety rules such as goggles and ear muffs when using machinery. Also insurance for when people are working with you.

Prospects for growth

There are a lot of competitors as the market for individually designed artwork is booming. People no longer want traditional products (such as cut crystal).

Tips for success

Don't be persuaded into accepting all commissions that come along. It may seem tempting to try and do everything but it's much better to pick the better ones as these will help build your reputation for quality.

Pros

Attending national and international shows can quickly build up contacts and colleagues in the business.

Cons

Establishing yourself as a known artist can take time.

Useful contacts

Your local authority and trade or craft shows in your area

Information and tips on various craft businesses: www.craftsforum.co.uk

Cake making

What is it?

Creating cakes, often for special events such as weddings and birthdays. You'll be buying, weighing, measuring and mixing ingredients and many cake makers also offer cake-decorating services, including piping, crimping, sugar and marzipan coating.

What's the appeal?

It's ideal for those who enjoy practical work, have a good head for figures, are well organised and who have an interest in cookery and food. A sweet tooth is essential too as you'll be testing and tasting every cake you make.

What skills do I need?

Patience, creativity and steady hands, particularly if you specialise in cake decorating. You don't need any specific qualifications but training can help make your cakes look professional and stand out from the crowd. There are plenty of courses available in cake making and decorating, such as ones specialising in sugarcraft and marzipan techniques.

What does it cost?

Your start-up costs will depend very much on how big an operation you wish to run and whether you choose to do it from your home or hire out a kitchen. You should invest in a website to promote your services as many people now source cakes over the internet.

What can I earn?

Prices of cakes can vary widely, depending on the work that has gone into it and what ingredients are used. You'll have to factor in delivery costs as well as most cake business do their own deliveries. A simple, 10-inch cake can cost from £35, whereas a five-tiered wedding cake can be priced at £900 for example.

Any red tape?

Food hygiene and preparation rules apply to any premises in which food is prepared – even if it is your own home. The main regulations you will have to be aware of are Regulation (EC) No. 852/2004 on the hygiene of foodstuffs, and the Food Hygiene Regulations 2006. Although this one applies specifically to England, there are equivalents for Scotland, Wales and Northern Ireland. Research these carefully as there are a number of areas to watch out for.

Prospects for growth

Consider other services you can offer alongside cake making, such as home-made chocolates, to boost growth prospects.

Tips for success

Practise on friends and family as much as possible so you can try out different designs and tastes. Consider perfecting a small range of 'signature' cakes that will distinguish you from the competition.

Pros

Cakes are for celebratory occasions, so you can get a real buzz from seeing the finished product and satisfied customers.

Cons

Cake making is labour intensive so beware of taking too many orders – you may find yourself working round the clock to fulfil them.

Useful contacts

The Bakers' Federation: www.bakersfederation.org
Food Standards Agency: www.food.gov.uk

Jewellery making

What is it?

Earrings, necklaces, bracelets, precious stones, silver and gold – jewellery making includes all these and more. You could specialise in one-off custom-made pieces or design a collection for mass production.

What's the appeal?

It's a job that can be done easily from home and carried out at the hours to suit you, but it can also involve travel to trade shows and abroad to source materials.

What skills do I need?

There are many craft and jewellery making courses available – if you are completely new to the work, a course will teach you all the basics. In terms of skills, accuracy and attention to detail are a must and good negotiation skills will help when it comes to working with suppliers. For more expensive types of jewellery, you might need to learn soldering techniques.

What does it cost?

Making beaded jewellery has minimal start-up costs. You'll need to invest in basic tools such as beads, clasps, ribbon, wire, pliers and cutters, all of which can be picked up in craft and tool shops.

What can I earn?

Jewellery making can be a painstaking and time-consuming process so you should factor the time taken in any commissions, as well as the cost of materials. For individual pieces for example, work out the cost of time and materials and then double this to arrive at a price. For pieces sold in bulk, you can adjust the price as you will be producing identical pieces faster.

Any red tape?

There are no specific regulations but if you decide to sell your jewellery over the internet, phone, by mail order or digital TV, you'll need to comply with the Consumer Protection (Distance Selling) Regulations.

Prospects for growth

Consider selling your jewellery to retailers but do your research carefully and ensure your collection complements that of the shop in terms of style, materials used and pricing. Good quality photographs will also help to promote your business. Consider what makes it special, as this can form the basis of any marketing material. You might also want to consider offering an alterations or repairs service to expand your offering.

Tips for success

Buying your materials wholesale will help lower your costs, especially if some parts of your collection prove popular and generate repeat orders. Many materials such as silver and gemstones can be ordered abroad cheaply. In this industry, talent and contacts are key to getting work so attend as many trade shows as possible.

Pros

If you are using precious stones, you can combine a trip abroad with sourcing materials.

Cons

It can take time to establish yourself and your designs so you might need additional income from another job in the early days.

Useful contacts

Support for the craft and jewellery industry: www.thegoldsmiths.co.uk
Jewellery and Allied Industries Training Council (JAITC): www.jaitc.org.uk
Trade Association: www.bja.org.uk

Greeting card maker

What is it?

Greeting cards are used for many occasions, such as birthdays, weddings and anniversaries and for seasonal events such as Easter and Christmas. There are two options when starting a business in the greeting cards industry: you can either become a greeting card publisher or supply existing greeting card publishers with your artwork and receive a fee for this.

What's the appeal?

Whether you write or design the cards, this job appeals to those who are creative. It can easily be run from home so can be fitted around other jobs and commitments.

What skills do I need?

A flair for design, art and words, together with basic computer skills. Depending on the type of card, a sense of humour can help too.

What does it cost?

The more expensive route is that of a greeting card publisher, as you'll need to factor in costs such as production, selling and administrative responsibilities. The more common and cheaper route is to supply existing card publishers with your artwork. You'll need paper and card to show your designs, which entails a minimal cost. Be prepared to travel to trade fairs and to various publishers to showcase your work.

What can I earn?

Earnings for writing and designing greeting cards vary enormously depending on the publisher, the design or writing you are proposing and the type of card, but you can expect to earn between £25 and £125 for one card.

Any red tape?

There are no specific regulations but be aware of copyright rules and licensing. The latter for example enables others to use your designs or images on their products, while you keep control of the copyright and get a guaranteed fee and/or royalty based on a percentage of product sales.

Prospects for growth

Writing and designing greeting cards is a part-time business, but if you build up enough contacts in this area, it can generate a good income, albeit a side one.

Tips for success

Do your research carefully – visit card shops to see what styles and sizes are popular and if there are any gaps in the market that you could cater to. There are plenty of trade shows for greeting cards where you can make contact with publishers. Think about the size and shape of the cards as this could have an implication on postage costs and on whether shops are likely to display them.

Pros

This work can be done in hours to suit you so you can invest as little or as much time as you want.

Cons

It's a very competitive business so it can take a while to receive your first commission or to secure regular work from publishers.

Useful contact

Trade association: www.greetingcardassociation.org.uk

Dressmaker

? What is it?

It involves making a variety of made-to-measure clothes – not just dresses – according to customers' individual requirements. You'll be measuring customers, organising fittings, giving advice and helping to choose fabrics and designs. You'll develop customers' measurements into patterns, lay this out on fabric and then cut around the pattern before stitching it together. Some dressmakers offer additional services such as alterations and repairs.

✓ What's the appeal?

Items you create are always original ones so the job can be immensely satisfying as you are creating something from scratch.

🔍 What skills do I need?

An interest in sewing and fashion, along with nimble fingers. As you will be giving advice on designs and creating patterns, imagination and creativity are a must too. You need to have an eye for visual effect and an interest in the latest fashion trends.

£ What does it cost?

You would need a sewing machine, which costs from £100 to £2,500 depending on its features. You'll also need basic equipment such as measuring tapes, cutting scissors, pattern makers, needles and thread. More intricate work will be finished by hand, and you might need beads and embroidery.

£££ What can I earn?

This varies according to what you are making but as a general rule, dressmakers can expect to earn between £220 and £270 a week, but this could rise to around £350 a week.

Any red tape?

There are no specific regulations but ensure you draw up a contract for costly jobs, or those where you will be dealing with expensive materials, such as wedding dresses.

Prospects for growth

It can take time to create an outfit for a client as it can involve several fittings so progress initially can be slow. Gauge how long it will take you to complete outfits so you can increase your bookings as the business grows, rather than taking on too much to start with.

Tips for success

You could choose to specialise in one area such as bridal wear so you can perfect your skills or dressmaking techniques. Joining a recognised body will also help to boost your profile, while word of mouth can be vital for bookings so ask your customers to spread the word if they are happy with your work.

Pros

You can carry out the work easily in your own home and it can be very satisfying when you see a creation become reality.

Cons

You'll need to be able to concentrate for long periods of time, as much of the work is methodical and intricate. You'll spend a lot of time sitting down or bending over and you may have to work weekends and evenings to meet deadlines.

Useful contacts

Professional association: www.textileinstitute.org
Tips on careers in fashion: www.canucutit.co.uk

Costume designer

What is it?

You will research, design and develop costumes in a range of styles such as period or country, mainly for use in movies, the theatre, television, concerts and for stage companies. You will be expected to create drawings and perhaps come up with a budget, and on occasion make the costume themselves.

What's the appeal?

Costume design is a creative job – you'll be responsible for taking an idea from concept to a tangible reality, which can offer good levels of satisfaction. You might be required to travel to different sets and even go abroad if necessary.

What skills do I need?

You'll need a high level of design skills, sewing ability, creativity, an understanding of materials, a good head for figures and be comfortable liaising with people as you will need to ensure you are responding correctly to a brief. You might also have to schedule fittings so organisation skills are important too. Many costume designers have a postgraduate qualification in costume design, fashion or theatre design.

What does it cost?

There are minimal set-up costs involved as all of the materials needed will be supplied by your clients. You should have basic tools such as a measuring tape, pattern cutters and scissors so you can work on designs at home.

What can I earn?

Rates vary widely depending on your experience and the production you are working on. According to the Broadcasting Entertainment Cinematograph and Theatre Union (BECTU), costume designers working on UK film and television productions within a 40-mile radius of central London can expect to earn around £721 for a 40-hour week.

Any red tape?

Ensure you protect yourself with professional indemnity insurance and are aware of health and safety regulations if you are working on a set.

Prospects for growth

Earnings in film and television are generally higher than those for theatre, but it's a hard market to break into. Costume design is a job, however, where the majority of people work freelance or from contract to contract so you would not be competing too much with those in permanent positions.

Tips for success

If you are new to the sector, get relevant experience by contacting local schools and amateur theatre groups to see if they need any help with costume design for plays and musicals. You'll probably have to offer your services for free but it can help you to build up a portfolio that you can share with potential clients. Costume designers tend to specialise in either theatre or in film and television.

Pros

The variety of the work involved, particularly if you choose to work across different mediums.

Cons

The hours are likely to be long, particularly in the run-up to shows. Designs might need to be changed at the last minute so you'll need to have bags of patience and flexibility.

Useful contacts

BECTU: www.bectu.org.uk
The Costume Society: www.costumesociety.org.uk

8

Entertainment

Profile – Acting coach
Who: Lucy Appleton
What she does: Acting coach
Where: Various locations across the UK
Set-up business: 2006
Initial start-up costs: Minimal

Preparation and creativity are two of the most important skills needed for an acting coach, according to Lucy Appleton, who has been working in this profession over the last two years. Originally from Boston in the US and with a background as an actor, casting director, researcher and editor, she has had plenty of experience, but she believes that personal skills are as important as practical ones.

'I've trained with some of the best teachers in the US and UK but you need to have a degree of critical thinking,' she says. 'This will enable you to justify what might seem to be unforgivable qualities in actors, allowing them to play parts without judging. I prefer to pepper criticism with positive feedback.'

Lucy has built up the business using contacts she made as an actor and casting director on both sides of the Atlantic. Since she has established her business in the UK, she has seen demand for her line of work grow.

In terms of start-up costs, no real outlay was necessary in Lucy's case, as all that she has needed and used is a workspace. One could set-up a studio, run workshops and hold regular classes, but she prefers to work on a one-on-one basis.

She charges by the hour and rates vary depending on the project. Many of her customers have come to her through word-of-mouth, an important way to promote yourself in the acting coach business.

In a typical week, she teaches two two-hour sessions a day, helping working actors to get more out of each performance through detailed script and character analysis. A huge amount of preparation goes into each lesson, including reading, rereading, researching and inventing exercises – all of this needs to be turned into a coherent lesson plan. She tends not to teach more than thirty hours a week, as she believes it would be unfair on the students, due to the amount of preparation required.

'Lesson plans are not gospel though,' she adds. 'There are many times when I have had to teach by relying on instinct rather than structure. Being an acting coach means you have to think spontaneously and not be frightened by the unknown or the untested. It's what makes the role exciting.'

Lucy says that empathy is a must too – any acting coach needs to have the ability to understand and feel for the person they are working with. A personal touch is important and it helps you to form a connection with each clients. Discretion is vital too – Lucy does not discuss her clients with anyone and does not use her client list for marketing purposes.

'You have to keep an open mind and know that, with guidance, even the weakest actor can improve. Honesty is perhaps the best way to gain a client's trust and is an important tool for creating a rapport,' she says.

According to Lucy, the best aspect of being an acting coach is seeing the look on someone's face when they are inspired to see something in a new light.

'I love my job and being able to help people and change the way they see or approach things makes all the hard work worthwhile,' she says. 'Also, I can choose how many hours I want to work so my earning potential is limitless.'

Her biggest challenge to date has been maintaining a client base without advertising. Lucy previously studied with an acting coach who never advertised his services and had an unlisted telephone number – yet his classes were full.

For those looking to become acting coaches, Lucy says the following are essential: you need a sense of humour, imagination and the ability to stop taking yourself too seriously. Lucy is based in London but often has to travel to where the work is, which involves being on location with actors all over the UK and working weekends and evenings.

Being an acting coach also involves a remarkable amount of patience and the desire to receive by giving – consequently, she believes it is not a job for everyone.

'You also need to be able to work flexible hours and have the support and understanding of friends and family,' she believes. 'And my job is never done – my work relies on techniques that are constantly evolving. You never stop training as there is always more to learn.'

Photographer

? What is it?

You can earn a living from various types of photography, but wedding photography is one of the most high-profile money-makers, particularly during the summer months. Other photographic options include passport pictures and portrait photography, and you could also specialise in corporate work, such as PR photo shoots.

✓ What's the appeal?

Photography is a creative skill, suited to those who like people and who enjoy trying to make them feel at ease.

🔎 What skills do I need?

As well as having a good eye for a photograph, patience is vital, particularly if you are photographing young children. A friendly and warm personality helps to put people at ease. Get some training and qualifications – there are plenty of courses covering portrait and wedding photography and they will help boost your credentials.

£ What does it cost?

Many home-based photographers convert a garage to provide an all-in-one studio, admin, storage and reception facilities. Budget around £5,000 for your conversion costs. Alternatively you can rent a small shop with a display area and a small studio, prices vary depending on your location. You will also need photographic equipment – a reasonable camera and lens, studio lights and backdrops should cost up to £5,000.

£££ What can I earn?

Potential earnings depend on many different factors, not least your range of services and your ability to market yourself as a top-notch photographer. A wedding can generate profits of anything between £50 and £750, while a portrait may generate between £30 and £500. Many photographers earn around £20,000 a year.

Any red tape?

Make sure you're fully insured – accidents and mistakes do happen. Talk to your local insurance broker about professional indemnity, public liability and product liability insurance.

Prospects for growth

Experiment as much as possible, for example taking pictures of a relative's wedding, so you have some experience of handling photography. An easy, risk-free way to break into the profession is to approach established wedding photographers listed in Yellow Pages and ask for a Saturday job.

Tips for success

Finding work as an assistant photographer is a good way of gaining experience, building your portfolio and learning on the job. Add web design to your capabilities or restoration to old or damaged photos as a way of adding value to the customer and increasing your return.

Pros

Weddings aren't going out of fashion so there is always work available, as long you distinguish yourself from the competition.

Cons

Wedding photography is seasonal – May to September is the busiest time so you'll need to supplement your income in the winter months.

Useful contacts

Association of Photographers: www.the-aop.org

British Institute of Professional Photography: www.bipp.com

Community site and database for assistant photographers: www.photoassist.co.uk

Gift baskets

What is it?

A home-based gift basket business involves arranging products such as baby items, food and bath and beauty products into baskets. You can make the containers for the products yourself or buy them, and the baskets can be sold to individuals or to companies. They are often designed for special occasions or seasonal times of the year such as birthdays, anniversaries, Christmas and Easter.

What's the appeal?

If you are creative and enjoy browsing shops for unusual gift items, this job could be ideal.

What skills do I need?

Creativity and an eye for design is essential as presentation can make all the difference in this job, making even the most ordinary of contents stand out. You'll need to have a flair for arranging items as gift baskets are often judged on their appearance first and contents second.

What does it cost?

You'll have to factor in expenses such as packaging and postage costs alongside the actual price of the items you are putting into baskets. You can choose to run this business over the phone and take credit card payments or you can set it up online, which will incur additional costs.

How much can I earn?

This will depend on whether you operate on a local, national or international basis and what kind of products you choose to sell. Your potential profits will also be influenced by whether you will be sourcing hard-to-find unusual items, or ones that can be more easily bought. As a general rule, you should mark up what it costs you to make up the basket by two or three times.

Any red tape?

You'll need to comply with the Consumer Protection (Distance Selling) Regulations which cover businesses that sell to consumers by mail order, phone, fax, over the internet or on digital TV.

Tips for success

To keep costs down, look for suppliers of inexpensive baskets – you can then make these look special by using ribbons and other decorative materials. You could even try spray-painting baskets different colours to fit in with a particular theme, such as green and red for Christmas. Think about the size and shape of the gifts you are selling before you buy the baskets.

Prospects for growth

This type of business won't be a big money-spinner but it can help you generate extra income.

Pros

It can easily be run from your home and at hours that suit you – as long you fulfil orders on time.

Cons

Delivering gift baskets in person is often the best and most memorable way for someone to receive them as you won't need to wrap it all up, but this can be time-consuming if you do this yourself and will restrict the areas you choose to market to.

Contact

Information on regulations: www.businesslink.gov.uk

Event planning

What is it?

Firms spend millions of pounds each year hosting conferences, running charity events, organising product launches and hosting company parties. To ensure the occasion runs smoothly, event planning companies are often brought in to run the behind-the-scenes show. If you want to target individuals, typical jobs include organising a wedding or a birthday party.

What's the appeal?

It's a business that demands an outgoing and sociable personality as you will be liaising with a lot of people at one time. You'll get to visit lots of venues so it's ideal if you like to travel.

What skills do I need?

A flair for arranging activities for friends and work colleagues is a good start, but many people who work in event planning have a background in events and catering for example, so it might be worth taking the time to do a course.

What does it cost?

The barriers to entry for start-ups are very low, with little initial outlay and no professional qualifications or association memberships required to begin trading. Essentially, you need a telephone, a car, some stationery (budget for around £500) and a PC. Most of your time will be spent talking on the phone.

What can I earn?

The main market to focus on is the corporate one as it has budgets to spend, although these are likely to be reduced in the face of the current economic downturn. A lot of revenue will be commission-based, so the more extras you bolt on, the more you will earn. Booking a venue can result in a commission of between 8% and 10% and you can then charge a flat fee for any add-ons such as catering and lighting, depending on customer requirements.

Any red tape?

There are no specific rules but you'll need to carry out a risk assessment regarding any catering services and venues you source/provide, by being aware of health and safety regulations as well as ensuring that the event itself meets required standards.

Prospects for growth

Competition in event planning is strong so you will to be motivated and maintain a positive attitude. To increase your business profile, make lists of companies in your local area and cold call to get some appointments. Keep a sales diary and contact businesses every couple of months or so to generate repeat business and to look for new opportunities.

Tips for success

Concentrate on specific areas, rather than provide the whole gamut of services, where you will hit a lot more competition.

Pros

As most of your work will be carried out over the phone, event planning can easily be run from home.

Cons

Event planning is a seasonal business so your income will run in peaks and troughs. The autumn and winter months are likely to be your busiest, in the run up to Christmas.

Useful contact

Meetings Industry Association: www.mia-uk.org

Children's birthday party organiser

? What is it?

You will plan a child's birthday party from start to finish, often creating a tailor-made event depending on the child's and parents' requirements. You'll be expected to give advice on party themes and styles, provide the decorations and food and be responsible for booking any entertainment such as a magician. Themes can vary from action and adventure, to cooking to craft parties. If the party is not held in the parents' home, you'll need to be able to source appropriate venues.

✓ What's the appeal?

Organising children's birthday parties can be very stressful so the idea is that you take away some of this stress from the parents. You must like working under pressure and with children, so the work suits those who are flexible and who have bags of energy.

🔎 What skills do I need?

You must be brimming with ideas and creativity as well as having good communications skills to deal with both children and adults. You'll need to be calm under pressure and have painstaking attention to detail as well as time management skills. The job involves dealing with many different points of contact so organisation is a must.

£ What does it cost?

Costs are minimal – you'll need a great contacts book so you can source suppliers quickly and easily.

£££ What can I earn?

Potential earnings depend on location and exactly what you offer. Children's birthday parties generally last for two hours and typical charges are £50–£75 an hour, but if you offer entertainments, decorations and catering services as part of your package, you can charge more or charge per child. As a general guide, charges per children are around £12.

Any red tape?

There are no specific regulations but as you will be working with children, it's a good idea to be aware of any health and safety rules. If you source venues, they need to be appropriate for use by children.

Prospects for growth

Word of mouth is very important in this type of business so ensure you gather testimonials from satisfied customers and ask them to recommend you.

Tips for success

Always plan for the unexpected where children's parties are concerned, such as extra guests or suppliers cancelling at the last minute.

Pros

Seeing satisfied parents and children can be immensely rewarding. As birthdays are celebrated all the time, demand for children's birthday parties is strong.

Cons

It can be a very time consuming job so it's easy to go over the 9am–5pm routine and work evenings and weekends. Any changes will need to be run past parents and you'll also need to be prepared to deal with any last-minute requests from them.

Useful contact

List of children's party organisers: www.angelsandurchins.co.uk

Children's entertainer

What is it?

It involves performing a variety of acts, usually at parties or special events. Acts include magic tricks and illusions, juggling, storytelling, singing and dancing and balloon sculpting. You could perform in a wide range of venues, such as people's homes, pubs, schools, restaurants and playgroups.

What's the appeal?

This job is suited to those who like working with children, who are outgoing and who are creative – much of the time, you will need to write your own material and devise your own act.

What skills do I need?

There are no formal qualifications required, but you will need to have a love of performing as well as lots of patience and energy. A sense of humour is also helpful and you should enjoy being the centre of attention. Training in music, dance or acting can also be a bonus, as is a driving licence.

What does it cost?

Depending on the type of act you perform, you will need to provide your own costumes and props. The costs for these will vary depending but props can be reused time and again at different events, so the initial outlay can be minimal.

What can I earn?

Incomes from children's entertaining vary enormously as much of the work is part time and it depends on the type of acts you are providing and over what time. As a rough guide, earnings per performance start from £50 and can go up to £200.

Any red tape?

You will need to be aware of relevant legislation regarding working with children and health and safety.

Prospects for growth

This is not a business where you can earn big money but you can look to charge extra if you work at weekends and evenings.

Tips for success

Keep up to date with the latest news and trends so that your material remains fresh and in demand. The more skills you have or develop, the more likely you are to find regular work. Word of mouth can be a good way of building contacts so ensure you get recommendations from one venue to the next.

Pros

Working as a children's entertainer is a source of income that can be fitted around other jobs, so you can make as much or as little as you have time for.

Cons

Working hours are likely to be irregular, as a lot of the work will take place in the late afternoon and early evening. You could spend a lot of time travelling, practising and rehearsing, which can be tiring and you'll need to maintain your own costumes and props.

Useful contacts

Creative and Cultural Skills: www.ccskills.org.uk
The Magic Circle: www.themagiccircle.co.uk
Arts Council: www.artscouncil.org.uk

Catering

? What is it?

Providing and delivering food and drinks to the customer's premises in return for a fee. This will often be for corporate clients who need food for board meetings, events, conferences and training courses. Private sector clients might include special occasion catering such as weddings, birthdays, funerals and anniversaries.

✓ What's the appeal?

It's a chance to work more flexibly and independently than you would be able to in a restaurant or café and obviously to be the boss.

🔍 What skills do I need?

As well as being interested in catering you really need a background in food so you have a feel for the basics such as supply and costing. A high level of food safety standards is a must – you and all staff need at least basic food hygiene and food handlers' awareness certificates.

£ What does it cost?

It's possible to trade from home if your kitchen has been modified but you will need catering equipment including a large fridge/freezer (£1,000), a commercial microwave (£900) and vegetable preparation units (£1,000) as well as trays and utensils. To transport food you need to keep it less than 8°C which means you should be able to manage with insulated food containers for short journeys.

£££ What can I earn?

Clients are charged by the head according to the type of food they require. A cold buffet might be anything from £6 to £10 a head rising to up to £20 for a more substantial fork buffet. Full meals might be £30 and upwards, depending on what's involved.

Any red tape?

You must register with the local authority before starting to trade and be inspected by Environmental Health (for non-porous services and separate areas for hot/cold and raw/cooked food). With premises not previously used for catering, you need planning permission and must comply with numerous food safety regulations.

Prospects for growth

To grow the business you will need to go out and sell it. This means advertising, good word of mouth and cold calling – there are a lot of small firms which will be in competition with you.

Tips for success

If you lose a client it could simply be that they want to try someone new – this can happen. But make sure you know why and alter the menu regularly to guard against this.

Pros

The business can grow and grow with the assistance of favourable word of mouth recommendations.

Cons

Stringent rules and regulations must be observed at all times – you could be spot checked by Environmental Health at any time and potentially immediately closed down.

Useful contacts

Your Local Authority to register the business
The Mobile and Outside Caterers Association (MOCA) for advise and training courses: www.moca.org.uk/

Personal chef

What is it?

It involves shopping, cooking and preparing meals for one-off occasions, such as dinner parties, birthdays and corporate events, or making a set number of meals for individuals, enabling people to freeze or store them over a period of time. You might also be asked to serve the meals, organise a kitchen and clean cupboards and fridges or give advice and prepare foods for people with special dietary needs.

What's the appeal?

You'll need to enjoy preparing and cooking food to quality standard, as well as shopping for all the ingredients.

What skills do I need?

It helps if you are a qualified chef but a certificate in cookery skills will also impress clients as well as give you a taster of what to expect. Organisation skills are essential and you also need good listening skills as most personal chefs will do a consultation before starting any work, to assess their clients' requirements.

What does it cost?

There are very low start-up costs associated with being a personal chef as you can use most of your clients' cooking facilities and charge them for the ingredients.

What can I earn?

The amount you can earn will vary depending on location and the type of cooking you are doing, but you can expect to earn between £100 and £200 a day or charge between £15 and £25 by the hour.

Any red tape?

You will need a food hygiene certificate which covers safe food preparation and cooking methods and you should also take out public liability insurance. If you are cooking on other people's premises, you won't need a licence.

Prospects for growth

More and more people are employing personal chefs as an alternative to eating at top class restaurants, but competition is strong. Referrals from satisfied clients and word-of-mouth can boost your bookings so ensure you collect as many of these as possible.

Tips for success

Decide whether you want to specialise in preparing menus for dinner parties and other events or whether you want to offer your services to a set number of homes. Develop a range of recipes that you can show to prospective clients and practise regularly with family and friends. Consider shadowing someone who offers personal chef services.

Pros

People's taste in food differs so this job can offer you variety and plenty of creativity, as you can design many different menus and use seasonal produce.

Cons

The working hours can be long as you'll be preparing food throughout the day, overseeing the cooking and services as well as tidying up. People can be very fussy where food is concerned so you'll need to be able to take criticism.

Useful contact

Food Standards Agency: www.food.gov.uk

Bed and Breakfast

What is it?

Renting rooms in your own home and providing breakfast for travellers or those taking short breaks in return for money. You may want to cater for the luxury end of the market or aim your services at those on a budget.

What's the appeal?

Given that you are effectively opening your home to strangers, you are blurring the edges between your business and your home life so you need to be confident and happy with the arrangement.

What skills do I need?

Personality plays a big part in creating a B&B. It is a creative profession in that you have to enjoy cooking and making your accommodation as pleasant and welcoming as possible.

What does it cost?

Costs for converting your house will depend on what is needed. Buying an existing B&B is not cheap, as they are often in vast Victorian villas with numerous bedrooms. To purchase a commercial property, most banks can lend up to 70% of the purchase price although you'll need to present a thorough business plan. The kind of market you want to attract will determine how much you spend on furnishings. Once you're up and running, your costs shouldn't be that high as apart from utilities, breakfast should be your only major cost.

What can I earn?

How much you earn will in some ways depend on your financial situation upon going into the business and where your B&B is located. Local tourist offices should be able to advise you of the turnover levels and the visitor numbers for B&Bs in their area.

Any red tape?

Check with your local planning authority, given that you may be changing the purpose of the building from purely residential to business. The number of guests you can accommodate will determine whether or not you have to register with Environmental Health officers. Fire regulations also need to be met – at the very least you will need a fire extinguisher and fire blanket.

Prospects for growth

Operating a B&B is something of a lifestyle business, a job that many people will undertake with their partners.

Tips for success

Your need to have sufficient space so if you want to have a four-bedroom business you will probably be looking for a six-bedroom property so that you have enough space for yourself. You should try to keep a part of the house yours, ideally you need a bedroom, bathroom and a private sitting room. Signing up to bodies such as the local tourist board, the RAC and the AA can help boost your business' profile as well as giving you a set of standards to stick to.

Pros

You can do the beds in the morning, leaving the afternoons free.

Cons

The larger the business, the more you are likely to need help, which means paying wages and incurring more costs. If you are looking for a work/life balance, stick to a small operation.

Useful contact

Information and advice: www.bandbassociation.org

Mobile DJ

What is it?

As a mobile DJ, you can expect to travel to various venues and events to play music, taking requests from clients. Mobile DJs generally do not specialise in any particular genre of music but you'll need to provide your own equipment, set it up and dismantle it at the end of an event.

What's the appeal?

Many mobile DJs love music so the job gives them the opportunity to earn money doing something they truly enjoy.

What skills do I need?

You don't need any particular qualifications but a love of music is a must and you must be comfortable working and interacting with people. You must be prepared to play a lot of music that you might not choose to listen to by choice. An ability to entertain is essential, using music to ensure people have a good time. A good speaking voice helps too as you'll need to introduce your set and make announcements from time to time at events.

What does it cost?

You'll need a van to transport your equipment which should include amplifiers, speakers, microphones, turntables and lighting. A complete mobile DJ package can be picked up for around £500, with more sophisticated sets costing around £2,000. Building up a good music collection is a priority, as you can always add to your equipment depending on the type of function.

What can I earn?

Income varies depending on location and event but you can expect to earn between £50 and £300 a session.

Any red tape?

Public liability insurance will protect you in the event of any damage caused to a third party through accident or neglect, and cover varies from £2m to £10m. Some venues may require you to have at least £5m cover.

Tips for success

Competition amongst mobile DJs is strong so to make this business as viable as possible, you should aim to offer a wide range of music so you can cater to many tastes. Consider offering your services voluntarily to an established DJ – it might not earn you much to start with, but you'll pick up the necessary skills and useful tips fast.

Prospects for growth

Much of the work for mobile DJs is at weddings and children's parties so your music collection should cater for all age groups. If you do want to specialise for one age group or function, do your research carefully to gauge whether there is enough demand.

Pros

As much of the work takes place in the evenings or at weekends, you can fit this job around other commitments.

Cons

Mobile DJs generate most of their work from weddings so your busiest months are likely to be during the summer so it could be harder to find work in winter.

Contacts

Training: www.ccskills.org.uk
School of sound recording: www.s-s-r.com

Acting coach

What is it?

It involves teaching different acting styles and techniques, as well as the history and theory of drama. Acting coaches also specialise in breathing techniques, voice projection and camera work. They can also help students to write and direct performances, prepare them for auditions and entry into drama schools. Most specialise in film, television or theatre.

What's the appeal?

Working as an acting coach offers creativity, versatility and fun and is a business that can easily be run from home, although you will increase your chances of bookings if you are prepared to travel.

What skills do I need?

Acting skills and knowledge of different styles of acting. A teaching qualification helps although it's not essential, but most acting coaches will have a solid background in drama or acting. Good listening and communication skills are a must and many acting coaches have taken additional courses in body posture, movement, speech and language.

What does it cost?

Start-up costs are minimal as all you need is a room with some chairs, although the space should be fairly large as you may need a lot of room if the coaching involves movement and voice projection. Textbooks may come in handy and cost from around £10 upwards.

What can I earn?

For one hour, you can expect to charge from £20 upwards, most acting coaches will charge between £30 and £50 depending on location and what is required. If you have to travel, remember to add these costs on.

Any red tape?

There are no specific regulations but if you work for a school or other training institution they will want to carry out thorough background checks and you'll need to abide by any rules they have.

Prospects for growth

Working as an acting coach isn't a big money business but as a part-time venture, it can generate a worthwhile income that can be supplemented by other jobs.

Tips for success

Find out which schools in your area offer drama classes and consider advertising your services there. Contact your local theatres to see if you can promote your services there – you may be able to organise a few weekend workshops which will enable you to tap into new clients. Decide whether you want to specialise in coaching for television, film or theatre.

Pros

Work can easily be carried out in your own home and at hours to suit you, so it can be fitted around other jobs or commitments.

Cons

Be prepared to deal with people who may not be that talented but who still want to persevere with the craft. If you are coaching children, you may have to deal with very ambitious and pushy parents.

Useful contact

Training and careers: www.ukperformingarts.co.uk

Singing lessons

What is it?

Singing teachers offer singing lessons, vocal skills such as breathing exercises and musical theory. You can choose to specialise in different types of singing, such as jazz, pop, opera, classical or rock and also help people who are auditioning for musicals or plays, or students preparing for music exams.

What's the appeal?

You can easily run this business from home so it's ideal if you need to fit it around home commitments, although you'll increase bookings if you are prepared to travel to people's homes.

What skills do I need?

It's not essential to have a teaching qualification but many singing teachers have a music degree or a diploma in music, as well as musical skills and the ability to play a musical instrument. A good knowledge of singing styles is useful as well as good communication skills as you could be working with people of all ages and with different singing abilities.

What does it cost?

You'll need a room with chairs and must be prepared to use any musical instruments you specialise in, such as a piano, although if you have these already you won't need to add this as a cost. Up-to-date textbooks will be helpful and these cost from £10 upwards.

What can I earn?

Lessons are normally charged by the hour and fees vary depending on location and the type of work you offer, but you can expect to charge between £20 and £30 an hour with travel expenses on top.

Any red tape?

There are no specific regulations. If you register with a specialist music college to offer lessons, they will want to check out your background and references and you will have to abide by any criteria they set.

Prospects for growth

Offering singing lessons isn't a big money business, but if you are prepared to work anti-social hours such as evenings and weekends, you could increase your earnings and growth potential. Try tapping into local schools as many of them offer singing programmes for students, such as Singing Classroom (music to support the curriculum).

Tips for success

Word of mouth can help to boost bookings, especially if you build up a reputation for helping students to pass music exams, for example, or give extra tuition for auditions. You could also combine private tuition by working part time for a college. Consider targeting the corporate market – singing lessons are often used to help build confidence and encourage teamwork.

Pros

Offering singing lessons is a good source of extra income and you can choose how much time to devote and when you want to work.

Cons

The work can be intensive and therefore physically draining, especially if you offer one-to-one lessons.

Useful contacts

Training courses: Associated Board of the Royal Schools of Music: www.abrsm.org
Incorporated Society of Musicians: www.ism.org

DJ

What is it?

DJs play live music for audiences at live venues or on the radio, using a variety of formats such as vinyl, CDs or digital players and equipment including mixers and microphones. There are different types of DJing, including club, where you'll be playing music in bars or nightclubs, and radio DJing, where you will be presenting a show using a mix of chat and music.

What's the appeal?

As a radio DJ, you get to script your own show so it suits someone who is creative, outgoing and who likes talking. As a club DJ, you get the opportunity to mix your own sounds and use sound effects.

What skills do I need?

You don't need any particular qualifications bar a love of and interest in music, an outgoing personality and the ability to operate the equipment you will be using. As a club DJ, you could be using decks, mixers and lighting gear. For a radio show, a good speaking voice is helpful along with the ability to carry out interviews and it's a good idea to take a course in radio production.

What does it cost?

A good music collection is a must, which you can build up over time. Clubs will normally have their own equipment for you to use, but it helps if you have some of your own club DJing equipment such as turntables, speakers and headphones (which will cost around £200) as this will mean you can set up in just about any venue.

What can I earn?

Income varies depending on location, event or the type of show you are presenting. As a rough guide, average earnings are between £50 and £300 a session.

Any red tape?

If you want to work in clubs, public liability insurance will protect you in the event of any damage caused to a third party through accident or neglect, and cover varies from £2m to £10m. Some venues may require you to have at least £5m cover.

Tips for success?

Competition amongst DJs is strong. As a club DJ, check out the local bars and nightclubs in your area. Record a DJing session that you can send to radio stations as an example of your work. Success in this line of work depends very much on your reputation and ability to network.

Prospects for growth?

Club DJing involves working on a casual basis, but this could be lucrative if you manage to work several sessions at different venues over one weekend, for example.

Pros

Many DJing stints can be done at clubs abroad, giving you the opportunity to travel.

Cons

As a club DJ, you will be working long and antisocial hours. Breaking into radio DJing is extremely competitive, so you may find you have to take on antisocial shifts (such as late-night slots) when starting out or offer services on a voluntary basis to build up contacts.

Contact

Training: www.radioacademy.org

9

Essential facts

There's no denying the attraction of starting a home-based business. It can be an excellent way to be your own boss without facing high bills for renting office space. Generally, it does mean a better working environment for you, with no distractions such as office politics, no delays on public transport – and at home, there's only one person to make tea for.

Some of the suggestions in this book have hopefully both inspired you and shown you the diversity of businesses that can be started from home. In many cases, the start-up costs are minimal and you'll need little in the way of equipment besides a computer, internet connection and phone.

But simple as working from home sounds, there are many things you will need to consider to ensure that a home-based business is the right move for you.

Starting a business from home isn't for everyone. While it can provide flexibility, if you're poorly organised it may not be for you. Some aspects are very much tied in with individual personalities, such as levels of self-motivation, your ability to deal with loneliness and isolation, and the family situation you find yourself in. Questions to ask yourself include: have you assessed the potential impact on your family and are you creating the most conducive environment for work? Do you have the mindset and discipline to work from home?

Other considerations apply to all businesses, regardless of your personality or the sector you choose. For example, as a homeworker, a good working relationship with a bank manager is essential. You need flexibility so that when the promised cheque fails to arrive, there is some understanding and not merely a curt letter with a 'fine' for exceeding your overdraft limit.

Equally when things are going well, you need some sound advice on handling your money – where to go for the best interest, how to make the most of moving money around in your accounts and how to raise some extra capital if necessary. As well as keeping on top of your finances, you need to ensure that you are staying on the right side of the law in terms of fulfilling tax, health and safety and insurance obligations – working from home does not mean skimping on the legal regulations that apply to non-home-based businesses.

The following pages contain all the essential facts about starting a business from home, including what to consider before taking the plunge, how to organise your office space, issues with planning permission, what insurance you need and where to get it, dealing with expenses, tax implications, health and safety, and how to get the right equipment for your needs.

Is a home-based business right for you?

Separating work and home life can be a challenge at the best of times, and this is even more pronounced for those who work from home. The emotional side of running your own business should not be underestimated and before you commit, consider the following scenarios.

Self-motivation

Imagine a warm, sunny day, no deadlines and a day to fill. For those with office jobs, there is no debate. Come rain or shine they must make their way to the office for the obligatory seven or eight hours.

It is slightly different for homeworkers. Without an immediate deadline, it is far too easy to put off what can be done today until tomorrow. The sunny day beckons and before you know it you are calling friends and planning a day out.

This is not the best way to approach a home-based business. Yes, working from home does allow for freedoms not granted to others – after all, that is why we put up with the hassle of dealing with the taxman and juggling several roles at the same time. But self-motivation is crucial.

One way to tackle this potential problem is to set aside certain days of the week as work days – regardless of other temptations. Do not book the carpenter to work that day, do not book a hair appointment and definitely do not go to the beach.

Use those days to find work if you do not already have a sufficient amount booked, catch up on the paperwork or organise your desk.

Those who have strict deadlines to meet might find it easier to plan ahead and to motivate themselves but there will be something that works for everyone. An artist might be able to use the promise of others admiring finished work, while others might use the lure of receiving payment.

It is also very easy to let self-motivation slip. It is often said that the beginning of the second year is one of the hardest periods for any start up. The first months are filled with enthusiasm and usually come with the blessing of financial backers. The beginning of the second year can see the end of the contract that made the move into self-employment worthwhile. It can also see an end to the year's grace from the bank. This can be a hard time to get through – and without self-motivation, almost impossible. It is vital to remember the reasons why you started in the first place and use those to see you through any tough times.

Loneliness and isolation

You are all fired up and ready to go. The order books are brimming and the future looks rosy. So why do you feel so miserable? Why is getting out of bed each day so difficult?

After a career in an office or even after a few years at college, home can become a very lonely place. Staring at the same four walls without relief can be wearing on the strongest of people but add in a few other problems and working at home can turn into a nightmare.

As with self-motivation, dealing with loneliness and isolation is very much an individual issue and something that only you can learn to cope with in your own way. But it is something to bear in mind when starting out. Think about your lifestyle before the business launch. Is this something you want to maintain?

If you need that constant human contact, factor it into your working day – a mid-morning chat with the postman or courier is hardly likely to bring total relief but calling in to see a client may make the difference.

Expect a large telephone bill as you call around your regular contacts. Keep in touch with old work colleagues – you never know when they may be able to help pass work your way and it also provides a link with the outside world.

Have someone to talk to at the end of the day and do not be afraid to contact small business organisations for advice. Groups like the Home Business Alliance (tel 0871 474 1015) and your local Business Link (www.businesslink.gov.uk) office will all be able to put you in touch with someone who can advise you. As the old saying goes, a problem shared is a problem halved – and talking through your problems can help cut the feeling of isolation.

Keep busy. Problems never seem so bad when you are tackling something else and after a day on the phone conducting business it is a relief to shut the door on the office and find a bit of peace and quiet.

The family situation

Family issues usually boil down to one problem – you are sharing your home lifestyle with your business. No matter who shares your home – or who doesn't – there has to be a balance between work and play. It is vital that you do not shut people out of your new world.

It is equally vital that they respect your space when you are working and do not sprinkle the day with interruptions about the faulty washing machine, ask you to pick up some shopping or collect the dry cleaning.

If you set aside certain days or hours for work, insist that they are respected. But that goes for you too. It is no good insisting that the office is a no-go zone all day and then, when it is time for family in the evening, you spend a few hours just popping into the office to finish something off.

If work spills into playtime, apologise to those around you and try to minimise the impact. This is the kind of issue that soon grows out of all proportion and causes real family strife.

Partners need to be part of the deal. Discussing business is easy for some and difficult for others but is often essential as a way of blowing off steam at the end of a hard day – this goes for homeworkers too. Without the office banter to provide light relief, working alone can build up pressures.

Use your partner as a safety valve but, of course, in moderation. They may have had a tough day too. Make sure they are happy with where you work and are able to respect your need for peace and quiet during office hours. You cannot expect to work in isolation if you do the paperwork at the kitchen table.

Checklist – Preparing for a home-based business

- Draw up a schedule and designate certain days of the week as work days to guard against distractions

- Remind yourself of the reasons you set up the business at regular intervals, such as every six months, so you can assess whether you are meeting your objectives

- Have someone to talk to at the end of the day, such as your partner, family or a business advisory service

- If you have a family at home, ensure you involve them with your plans for the business

- If you set aside certain days or hours for work, insist that these are respected by your family or others around you

Where to set up

It's important to consider where your office is in relation to the rest of your living space. Can you shut the door behind you and leave work behind? Do you want views of the neighbours' garden and the sounds of their kids? Does your office space impact on the family by depriving them of another bedroom, or a playroom?

You might be lucky enough to have a room in your house that is ready-made for an office space, such as a room converted into a study, but it's not uncommon for many entrepreneurs to have started out their business from their kitchen table or their bedroom. If you are serious about making a go of your home-based business, there are certain things to bear in mind to help you decide how best to organise your office space.

Whatever space you dedicate to your office, bear in mind that you will be inside this area from 9am to 5pm Monday to Friday and possibly longer, and perhaps at weekends too. It's important to try and give yourself a good view as it can help with the feeling of being connected to the rest of the world, as well as with inspiration. Ensure that the room is well lit and is warm in winter and cool in summer. It can be very lonely working from home and at least seeing the seasons change can help.

Try and make a space in a room where you can shut the door behind you at the end of the working day, as it's tempting to carry on working beyond the need to if you can't physically distance yourself from the office. Give yourself more room than you think you actually need – you will be surprised how quickly you can fill any given space and equally, how quickly such a space can become untidy. Projects can get completely buried in piles of paper and you can waste hours digging out that vital note.

With these points in mind, you need to decide whether to adapt an existing room or whether you are looking at converting the garage or shed outside – if you are lucky enough to have this option.

Using an existing space – the pros and cons

If you take up an existing room, consider other members of your family. Will they be happy to lose that space? If it has to impact on them, are they happy to keep out of the way while you are working and not interfere with the papers on your desk when you are not there? Ask anyone who has been working from home for a while and they will, almost without exception, say that separate space is vital. Fitting into a corner of a room may work if you are single but most partners, and definitely any children, will invade your space constantly if you try to share living space.

Consulting your partner is the key to making it all work. They must be happy to sacrifice the space. Remember that they could be under huge pressure in their own work and may not want to be reminded of the office when they get home. Finding your computer buzzing away in the corner might not be the best way to relax.

Equally if you are to lose the spare room, discuss the implications. Will you have to keep a bed in the room for Auntie Ethel's annual visit or could you manage with a sofa bed pushed to the back and rolled out on odd occasions?

If you are likely to have regular visitors to your business, working in a corner of the sitting room is not an option. It is not very professional to have to clear away last night's takeaway to create a space for them to sit down. You probably won't want to take them upstairs to a spare bedroom either.

If you anticipate a steady stream of visitors, then you will probably have to consider a completely separate space. This will involve a much higher cost. Many people convert a garage into an office, or put an office in the space above it. You will need to get quotes from local builders and also discuss the idea with your local planning office.

You may think that by converting a garage or outbuilding that you would automatically need permission but this is not necessarily so. If the building is not listed or does not have other convenanted restrictions and if it is for the 'incidental enjoyment' of the house, then you will not need permission in normal circumstances.

Planners generally do not object to offices at home but will have many more concerns if you are expecting to receive regular visitors or employ staff there. One of the biggest concerns is transport. Will visitors be parking their cars outside and blocking parking space for other residents? And if you need permission to build an office space, they will want to make sure you conform to health and safety regulations.

Also check the building costs and the time required for the conversion. Adding utilities such as lights, water and telephone lines can prove very costly if it is an entirely new installation.

Inside the office you will need dedicated telephone lines as well as a fax line and internet access. Again, plan ahead and try to envisage what your requirements might be in the future. Forward thinking can save a lot of unnecessary hassle later on.

Stand-alone office

Another option is to have an office at the bottom of the garden. Converting the children's disused Wendy house or the old garden shed is probably not the best idea but there are plenty of wooden 'offices' on the market.

Wooden structures do not necessarily need planning permission and can provide the answer to the space issue. But make sure you have adequate, safe heating as wooden huts can be notoriously cold in winter.

Most of us work alone and in many cases the need for staff only comes at a later stage as the business takes off. It might be best to rein in spending at the outset and try to balance your needs with the costs involved – now and in the future.

Giving yourself crippling start-up costs could set the whole business back by a couple of years at least and you may find that you really don't need anything more than a small office in the house.

Trial and error is a fairly good approach as long as you and any partner remain flexible. If it is not working, do not struggle on but think about what you need and try to remedy the situation.

The current situation in the housing market, where few people are planning to move, may mean that a house with dedicated office space is way beyond your reach. But for many homeworkers the decision to become self-employed is all part of a major lifestyle change – and this often includes moving home. When that happens, it is worth remembering that when you give all your requirements to estate agents. The list should read, for example, four bedrooms, a garden and, most definitely, one office.

Checklist – Setting up at home

- Whatever space you use, ensure it offers a good view and enough space to adapt to your business as it grows

- You should be able to shut the door on your office space at the end of the day so you are not tempted to work all hours

- Decide whether you want to adapt an existing room or convert a shed or garage – are there any planning permission considerations?

- Check whether there are enough facilities for your communications needs – both now and in the future

- Are you likely to receive visitors at your premises and if so, can you accommodate them?

Planning permission

When it comes to working from home, planning officers say there are no hard and fast rules. The key is to discuss any issues you have. Check with your local council about whether any proposed developments need planning permission.

Planning officers say it is all down to a case of material change in use and this is open to interpretation. If an individual uses a study or third bedroom working from home then there is no problem. But if they employ anybody or use a larger portion of the house, then they need to have a chat. Officers stress that this does not necessarily mean you will need permission but you would be wise to get in touch with them for advice.

The classic example that planning officers are taught at college is that planning inspectors work from home – they use one room as an office and this is deemed acceptable. The classic example of those who have to think more carefully are the likes of hairdressers or chiropractors who potentially would need permission.

Whether you need planning permission is determined by whether it is a material change of use; whether you get permission is determined by levels of activity and the type of use.

Much will depend on whether you employ others, or have regular visitors, or your business results in a notable rise in vehicles on the surrounding streets. If you are simply using a desk in the corner of a room, most councils are not concerned with specific planning permission. But if you are converting a barn or garage into a fully fledged office then, without doubt, they will want it done by the book.

For example, planning permission will usually be needed if your business takes over and alters the character of your home, so that it is no longer used substantially as a private residence. The impact on the surrounding residential environment is also taken into account, for example if your business involves any activities unusual in a residential area, it disturbs your neighbours at unreasonable hours and you employ workers at home who are not normally resident there. If you are in any doubt, contact your local council.

Part of any planning permission will include meeting the necessary health and safety requirements. Again, these will be tailored to your specific usage but this needs to be checked.

Checklist – Plan ahead

- Your local council should be your first port of call when in doubt over planning permission

- A key question to ask yourself is: has my home become a business premises first and a home second?

- Think carefully about whether you need the facilities that may result in having to go through planning permission

- Health and safety requirements in relation to planning permission need to be respected

- If you need to make structural changes to your home, they must meet the requirements of the building regulations, which are enforced by local authorities

Getting the right equipment

These days communication has to be the key for any homeworker. Relying on one telephone line for home and office alike is unlikely to be sufficient, nor does it come across as very professional. The vagaries of the postal service can also be a challenge, although it's still worth knowing which postbox has the latest collection time – after all, invoices will probably still travel by post.

Think very carefully about your communication needs – this is the one area where you may spend more money than makes sense to begin with but you will find that installing an extra phone line was very worthwhile. If you have teenage children, arguing over the phone bill will probably be part of your way of life – even with itemised billing. Once you start working from home, the telephone bill can become a serious bone of contention. Not planning properly from the outset can lead to greater costs being incurred in the future. If possible, have at least two lines into the house. This makes sense, not just for easier division of the bill, but also to avoid your children hogging the line when you are waiting for an important business call. It is also easier to have a second line dedicated to the business than to risk your toddler answering the call from your top, but very sensitive, client.

When it comes to phone and broadband contracts, there is so much competition for your business so it is well worth researching the best deal. Think hard about your actual requirements and then start calling a few providers. Several have good deals for those making lots of overseas calls, others sell packages of phone lines and some have preferential business rates that might suit a small start-up operation. Having decided on the service provider, you will need to consider the equipment. Do you need several different phones or will a cordless suffice? That way you can be out in the garden on a sunny day and not tied to your office, waiting for the phone to ring.

Most of us will not sit at our desk religiously from 9am to 5.30pm so it's likely you will need an answer machine or a divert facility. If you need a fax machine, perhaps it makes sense to buy a machine that also operates as a computer printer or scanner. However, if you are considering such a machine, check that the print quality will deliver and not leave you wondering why you did not invest in separate machines in the first place.

Mobile phones are another issue – think about what will happen when you are away from home. As many of us travel around a bit, we need that contact with our clients. Shopping around is the answer once more to achieve the best package – you should research at least three deals.

Equipment is not all related to technology and communications. Ensure you invest in a good chair and desk and fill your own stationery cupboard – your neighbour might lend you a cup of sugar but a spare stapler might be more challenging. Carrying out a risk assessment is also vital – health and safety officers enforce strict rules about electric cables running across office floors – you don't want to break a leg by tripping over the wire to your computer either.

Above all, don't forget the mechanics. Check that there are adequate power points for the computer, fax, printer, telephone and all the other equipment that you will need.

Organising your bills and expenses

Besides equipment, another and sometimes unexpected drain on your start-up resources are travel expenses. Even though you are working from home, there will often be a need to travel – whether this is simply a trip to the post office each day with your mail or flying off to exotic locations to meet a client.

Think about the up-front costs and how much you will be able to claim back. Some expenses you can charge to clients while others can be offset against tax, but you will need to fund them all yourself up front. Overall, none of these costs should impact too heavily on the business as long as you have factored them into your initial planning.

Checklist – Equipment needs

- Try to look beyond the present and think about what you might need in six or even 12 months' time. It's easier to install phone lines in one session rather than adding additional ones at later intervals

- Shop around for the best deals and ensure you get at least three quotes. Negotiate what works best for you as many packages are flexible

- Investing in the right furniture is as important as choosing the right technology – you need to feel comfortable and have space for storage

- Be aware of health and safety rules to minimise the potential for any accidents occurring

- Invest in an answer machine or answering service – you can't be expected to answer every call but neither do you want to miss a potential lead

Insurance: what you need to know

As homeworkers, it can be tempting to pay little heed to specific needs and many people simply rely on existing home contents and buildings insurance for example. But when something happens, it can be all too late to take any precautions so it's important to guard against being woefully underinsured.

Meeting health and safety regulations is considered standard by insurers. They may have some additional special requirements such as security. Even if you simply have a desk in the corner of a room, check with your insurers.

Most insurers will add on coverage for the business equipment at no extra cost in such a case but they will not pay out for any claim unless they were aware that you were operating from home.

If you have a mortgage on your home, check with the bank. Again, these days it is usually accepted without any problem because so many of us work from home but they will need to know. If you have a lease, you will need to call your landlord or check your lease. There is rarely a problem for homeworkers but landlords might be less happy if you suddenly attract a stream of callers to their house.

Tailored homeworker policies are available on the market from many specialist insurance companies. These packages will often include Employer's Liability Insurance (ELI) and Public Liability Insurance (PLI) as standard. If you are employing others, you must, by UK law, have ELI – even if you are working from home. A standard policy will add around £140 to your annual insurance costs. If you have a lot of expensive equipment, it will probably cost nearer £300 a year extra.

Even if you work alone, employing someone on a temporary or casual basis, such as a cleaner or holiday help would expose you legally and financially should that person injure themselves while carrying out a job at your request. If you do employ any staff in such a capacity, you need to ensure your business insurance covers it. However, if you don't employ any staff, check your policy to make sure you aren't paying for employer's liability insurance.

Optional covers, but worth considering depending on the nature of your business, are Public Liability Insurance (PLI) and Professional Indemnity Insurance (PII). PLI is relevant in case of a need to pay damages to members of the public for death, injury or damage to property or vehicles arising as a result of your business. A good example of a business needing this cover would be a family run bouncy castle business. You need to make sure you are paying for the right amount of cover. Some insurers will quote you for a level of cover of between £1m and £5m but you may only need £1m of cover. It is always best to shop around to make sure that you do not pay excessive premiums for a level of cover that you do not require.

PII protects against financial liabilities to third parties arising from acts that could be deemed negligent whilst operating your business. It is particularly important for tradesmen and professionals who give advice or manage aspects of other businesses, such as IT or accounts.

Neither PLI nor PII are compulsory but apart from the need to protect yourself and your business, you may find that you may have to provide proof of insurance in order to secure a job or client. Lack of the correct insurance could therefore impact on potential earnings.

Other insurance needs that you may decide to pay for would be premises insurance. While you would already have building and contents insurance for your home, it will not usually cover business operations.

If you are storing your stock at home then consider contents and stock cover. Tradesmen's tools are notoriously expensive, not just leaving you heavily indebted if they are stolen, but you could be risking loss of income if you cannot afford to pay for new tools or carry out work.

Don't forget car insurance – if you are going to use it for business, ensure that your insurance allows for this. Many comprehensive policies include this as standard, but if it's not specifically mentioned on your policy you'll need to get it added.

Sickness and accident

Many of the self-employed do not consider what would happen if they were unwell or had an accident that prevented them from working. Sickness and accident policies cover these eventualities but are normally only for the shorter term, hence the reason they are relatively cost effective. For longer term cover there is Income Replacement Insurance or Permanent Health Insurance. For many self-employed the costs associated with such policies are prohibitive.

The bottom line when running a business or working from home is that you must check all the fine detail and small print contained in the policies. Remember, most people are under-insured when it comes to buildings and home contents. Do not make the same mistake with your business. Most insurers are quite happy to include an element of business equipment on the home policy. The trick is to make sure they are aware of what you are doing. Non-disclosure is one of the most frequent reasons behind the refusal to pay out a claim. Insurers say they are always happy to assess a risk and provide the policy required – but they can only do this if they have the relevant facts to start with.

If you use a broker, give them a call. It may be that your existing household policy can be 'tweaked' to suit your needs at no extra cost or just for a small sum. It's important to shop around and to ensure you get the best and correct deal, so ensure you give all parties concerned the relevant details. There are policies available on the internet, through high street brokers and over the telephone. All the usual suspects of home insurers will be able to give you a quote, just check the fine print for inclusions and exclusions.

Health and safety at home

You'll need to carry out a health and safety risk assessment if you use your home as your workplace. This is to help identify any potential hazard to you, other members of your household and any visitors who may come to your home-based office.

There are many dangers in the workplace that apply equally to home-based businesses, such as electrical equipment, the risk of fire, loose cables or wiring that can lead to trips or falls and excessive noise. Carrying out a risk assessment involves evaluating whether a danger is significant and if it is, what precautions you have taken to reduce the risk. You don't have to keep written records of your health and safety assessment unless you employ five or more people.

Checklist – Are these issues covered by your policy?

- Do you have adequate cover for your expensive equipment?

- Can you take your equipment in the car or abroad and still be covered?

- What happens after a fire/flood/subsidence?

- What happens if a visitor has an accident?

- What happens to any staff after an accident?

- Have you checked your policy for any specific exclusions?

Tax: what you need to know

Working from home can affect your tax situation as any rooms in your property that you use for work could be subject to business tax rates rather than council tax. You will still have to pay council tax on the rest of your property; whether your local council charges business rates or not depends on the degree of business use. You are more likely to have to pay business rates if a room is used exclusively for business, or has been modified (such as a workshop). Each case is considered on an individual basis.

If you run a guesthouse or a significant B&B operation or make a holiday home available for rent, you may be liable to business rates. If you have set aside a room solely for working in, you may be liable for Capital Gains Tax if the property is sold.

Electricity, gas and water bills land on all our doormats with monotonous regularity. The situation does not change for homeworkers – except be prepared for higher than average bills. As you are there throughout the day, you will automatically use more heating, water and electricity. These oncosts can hit cash flow, so be prepared. On a more positive note, running a business from home enables you to claim tax relief on domestic bills for those areas of the house used for your business, but be careful not to be too greedy about this. If you claim too much, you potentially tell the taxman that your home is all about business and then, when you come to sell it, he may treat any profits made as capital gains.

If your business is VAT registered, you may be able to claim back VAT on articles you buy for business use. If you install a separate phone line for your business, it will be easier for you to claim tax relief on business calls. If in any doubt about your tax situation, contact your local Inland Revenue office, or speak to your accountant if you have one.

Business rates

Often called non-domestic rates, these apply to businesses and other organisations that occupy non-domestic premises. Whether or not your local council charges business rates or not depends on the degree of business use. Each case is considered individually, so if in doubt contact your local council.

Premises that are subject to business rates are given a rateable value by the Valuation Office Agency (VOA). These values are reviewed every five years, and the new values will come into force in 2010. Factors used to assess the rateable value include the size of the premises and how they are used.

Checklist – Tax issues

- Keep accurate records so you have the necessary paperwork when it comes to claiming tax relief

- Check your tax situation with your local Inland Revenue office

- Find out whether business rates apply to your company

- If your business is VAT registered, you may be able to claim back VAT on articles you buy for business use

- New rateable values come into force in 2010

Conclusion

In the current economic climate, starting a business from home is proving increasingly attractive and the suggestions in this book have hopefully given you the inspiration, ideas and knowledge to prepare you for the next step. Whether you choose to learn new skills, adapt your existing ones to a home-based environment or want to turn a hobby into something more permanent, you can join one of the many millions of people who have enjoyed success and found satisfaction in home-based businesses.

While we've covered all the essentials of starting a home-based business, if you're serious about turning your idea into reality, there are many other issues you'll need to be aware of. These include how to register a business, where to get funding, managing your finances, and sourcing suppliers. You'll also need to consider the best form of marketing for your business and how to target customers effectively. For information on all of these topics and more, there is plenty of additional advice available and we've put a few suggestions below. Our new book, *Start Your Own Business 2009: The Ultimate Step by Step Guide* (Crimson Publishing, 2009), is also packed full of tips and resources for budding entrepreneurs.

Where to go for additional advice

www.startups.co.uk
www.businesslink.gov.uk
www.hmrc.gov.uk
www.princes-trust.org
www.fsb.org.uk
www.start.biz